MW01626181

THE ENNEAGRAMS OF THE DIVINE FORMS

PERFECT, ETERNAL, UNCHANGING TRUTHS

THE ENNEAGRAMS OF THE DIVINE FORMS

PERFECT, ETERNAL, UNCHANGING TRUTHS

OSCAR ICHAZO

ISBN: 978-0-916554-98-9

© 2023, 2024 Oscar Ichazo. All rights reserved. Second edition.

No part of this book may be reproduced or utilized in any form or by any means, electronic or mechanical, including photocopying, recording, or by any information storage and retrieval system without permission in writing from the publisher.

Arica, Arica School, P-Cals, Protoanalysis, Psychocalisthenics, and *Universal Logos* are registered trademarks of Ichazo, LLC.

Trialectics is a trademark of Ichazo, LLC.

Published by The Oscar Ichazo Foundation, PO Box 645, Kent, CT 06757 USA www.arica.org

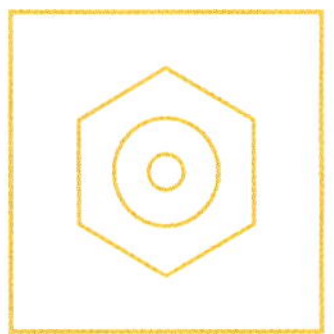

The Teachings presented in this book are offered for the benefit of all and the realization of a united humanity, Humanity–One.

Oscar Ichazo

CONTENTS

CONTENTS

ILLUSTRATIONS AND SUMMARY

OSCAR ICHAZO

FOREWORD

Oscar Ichazo's book, *The Enneagrams of the Divine Forms—Perfect, Eternal, Unchanging Truths,* begins with the scientific foundation upon which the entire Integral Philosophical Teachings are based. This leads into the connection to The Scarab and its Eighteen Spheres of Perception and Reality. Understanding the basis upon which the Divine Forms manifest is all–important since they determine how the 'Intellectual Principle in itself' is realized as the ground of the Creative Mind (Sphere 7) of The Scarab. The book clearly outlines how the Divine Forms are an integral part of the complete Theory of Integralism and how this builds a 'Theory of Knowledge,' that otherwise would be baseless.

The Divine Forms reveal Objective Reality, from which the entire material world is created. This Reality manifests from the Transcendental Mind of The Scarab (Sphere 1). Founded upon Integral Philosophy, the book provides a comprehensive perspective on the relationship of the Divine Forms to Protoanalysis, including the Mentational Analysis of the Divine Forms and a full description of the nine Fixations, the Trifix, and the ego–reduction of each Fixation; continuing into the Higher Absolute States with the Divine Energies, the Divine Forms, the Integral Virtues, the Divine Principles, the Divine Attributes, the Divine Gnoses, the Divine Names of God, and the Highest State of *Theosis* (Enlightenment).

The Enneagrams of the Divine Forms book exposes a substantial Teaching in which the study and practice with the Divine Forms opens Transcendental Knowledge beyond concepts and language into States of Perfection, Eternity and Innate Awareness.

Sarah Ichazo

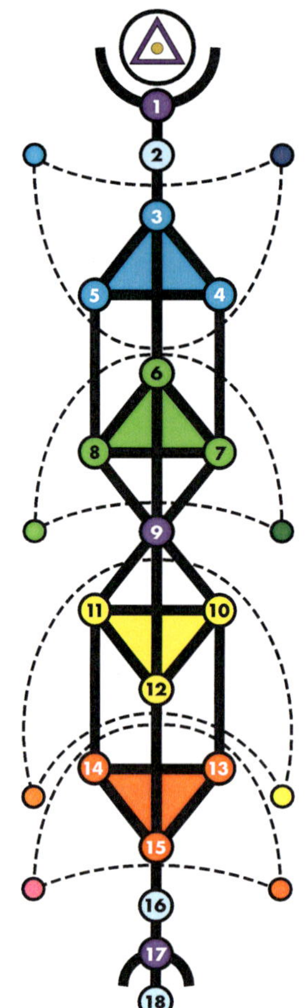

1 Transcendental Mind
2 Universal Mind
3 Ornamental Mind
4 Attributive Mind
5 Contemplative Mind
6 Illuminative Mind
7 Creative Mind
8 Volitional Mind
9 Enlightened Mind
10 Intuitive Mind
11 Analytical Mind
12 Intentional Mind
13 Functional Mind
14 Reactive Mind
15 Existential Mind
16 Primordial Mind
17 Cognitive Mind
18 Somatic Mind

THE SCARAB

CHAPTER 1

INTRODUCTION

In *De Anima* (On the Soul), Aristotle tells us in the most determinate proposition, but put in a casual and loose way, "All is Soul, so to speak." Integral Philosophy reaffirms this fundamental premise, asserting that, in fact, the Soul or the Sentient Being is a structure composed of an organic body with its organic systems, which is the foundation for a super–structure of another seventeen independent spheres (see The Scarab), each one with a distinct reality that functions in accordance with the Laws of Trialectics, or the logic of process in a reality that is cyclical.

In Integral Philosophy, the sphere of the body is described as the Somatic Mind (Sphere 18), since it is an organism that functions in a total way that shows an internal purpose, a teleology, or a finality, which is presented in all the functions and organs in three organic Systems and two endocrine Systems. For instance, the eyes show the appropriate structure for vision and, of course, the purpose of vision was pre–established and has the right design for accomplishing the function of seeing. The 'organism in itself' has one main purpose as a whole and that is the basic 'will to live,' which is the basic function of survival.

Aristotle tells us in the *Nicomachean Ethics* that all organisms have, as a primal function, the desire for the 'good in itself' and the maintenance of life. This fundamental organic function of survival, which is also called the 'will to live' in Schopenhauer's wording, the 'will to power' in Nietzsche's terminology, or the '*elan vital*' of Bergson, is based on the Heraclitean idea that the Essential Self of human beings was a 'celestial fire.'

This description was improved by the Stoics, who qualified this *fire* as the pure mind of clear awareness which, in fact, was Anaximenes's *pneuma* (Gk) or a 'spiritual air' that permeates our entire organism and our entire existence. It has been observed that this concept of a spiritual air permeating and sustaining all existence can also be found in the idea of *prana* (Skt) in the Hindu Traditions and practices. This whole organic body is the basis of the eighteen spheres of a super–structure (The Scarab) that constitute the human Soul in Integral Philosophy.

There are two basic levels in the human organism. In the first level, we find five main organic functions performed by five distinct Systems: three organic Systems (Digestive System, Circulatory System, and Cognitive System) and two Systems that relate to the Endocrine System—the Reproductive System and the Nervous System (containing the pineal gland which regulates the pituitary gland that controls the other endocrine glands by way of its tropins). In the second level, the five Systems function all together as one organism that forms Sphere 18 of the Somatic Mind of The Scarab.

The five organic body Systems of the Somatic Mind (Sphere 18) ensure the functioning of the organs and glands as five elements, the outcome of which, in Integral Philosophy, influences the determined states produced by the wavelengths of the different energies which manifest in the Cognitive Mind (Sphere 17). Two of these five Systems (Reproductive and Nervous Systems) manifest in the next Sphere (Sphere 16), known as the Primordial Mind, which contains the Sexual Pole that is the outcome of the male and female sexual organs (gonads) of the Reproductive System and promotes the Sexual Drive. This Mind also contains the Spiritual Pole which is the outcome of the Nervous System composed of the spinal cord, peripheral nerves, and the pineal gland and supports the Spiritual Drive. The Spiritual Pole, the other aspect of the perception and Knowledge of the Primordial Mind (Sphere 16), is the internal Drive toward Knowledge and the discovery of the outside environment, as another basic manifestation of the 'will to live.'

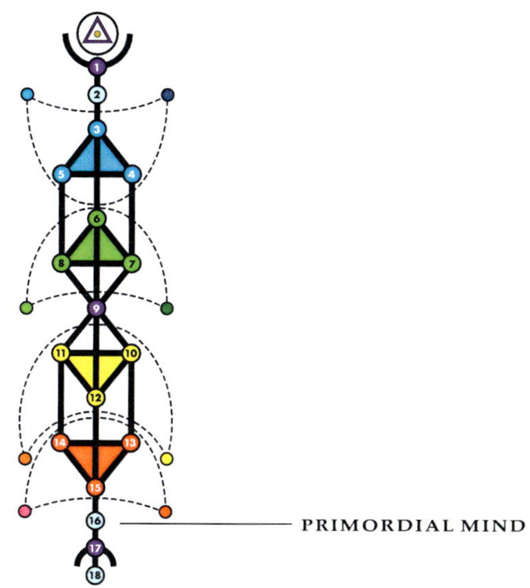

The Primordial Mind is then the deepest and purest psychic Sphere, because the Sexual Pole gives us the Drive of sexuality that is manifested in the Enneagram of the Sexual Pole. The Spiritual Pole gives us our primordial attitude toward life that we find at the moment of being born and during the period of lactation. If we feel as an infant that we are well received by a kind world, we can later posit our faith in the benevolence of the Cosmos in which we are born and, further on, we can believe in a God that is Good and accepting, giving us our spiritual strength and causing us to act under the belief that our actions will be well received by our society and accepted as the 'will of God,' who will give us providential support. This providential support depends entirely upon this, our first sense, in which the Spiritual Pole manifests as fundamental faith in The Good of the world. Otherwise, it will manifest as disbelief and distrust of an aggressive and cold society, leaving us, when starting any interchange at the social level, with an aggressive, narrow and distrustful attitude finding ourselves incapable of establishing internal roots for believing in a Good God.

The basic tensions of survival form over these two Poles of the Primordial Mind, sexuality and spirituality. The Sexual Pole manifests the Drive of physical survival, which is all–important for a balanced and healthy sexuality, indicating the personal drive for survival in the material world. The Spiritual Pole manifests the drive of spiritual survival which in our present life develops in the form of a faith in society, in God, and in oneself. Because of this, the Drive of spiritual survival will, in final terms, search for immortality and what is beyond the material world. Thus, gender and faith will define the characteristics of our Primordial Mind or our primordial perception of the world as matter and as Spirit, and it is upon this primordial conception of matter and Spirit that develop the Poles of our entire psychic life—the Soul with its structure of eighteen distinct Spheres of Perception and Reality. Two of these Spheres (Somatic, 18 and Cognitive, 17) are organic and material, Spheres 16 to 10 are relative in nature, Spheres 9 to 2 are

Absolute, and Sphere 1 is Transcendental.

Above the Cognitive Mind (Sphere 17) of the organic Systems, we find the Primordial Mind (Sphere 16) of the two Poles or Drives of survival, which are those of the material and spiritual that develop into the Existential Mind (Sphere 15), the fifteenth mind in the series of The Scarab. The Existential Mind is composed of three Instincts.

THE CONSERVATION INSTINCT

First is the Conservation Instinct which covers survival at a physical level and which is conservation of the body through food, drink, shelter, and all sorts of material goods related to our conservation as a feeling persona or ego.

Second, there is the Relation Instinct or our instinctual need to relate to our society in order to survive, which produces an emotional persona or ego; it is our relations with other human beings upon which our emotions depend.

Third, the Adaptation Instinct is related to the Cognitive System and manifests the instinctual inclination to know and work with our environment, either natural or human, to obtain

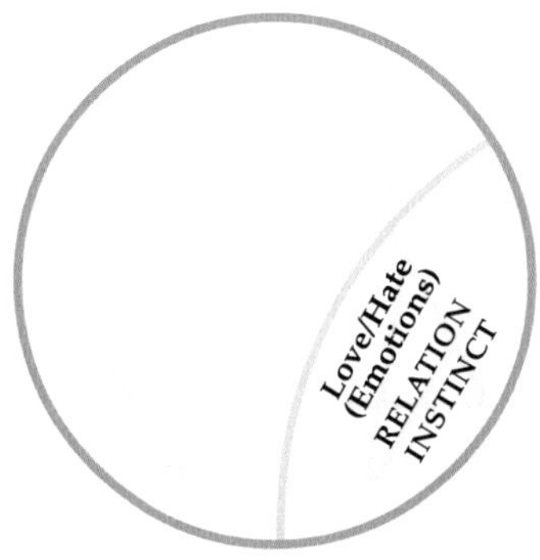

THE RELATION INSTINCT

the means for our survival. This Instinct is based upon a discriminative mind that tends to adapt its natural and cultural environment to the purpose of its own survival or whatever means survival for this intellectual persona or ego.

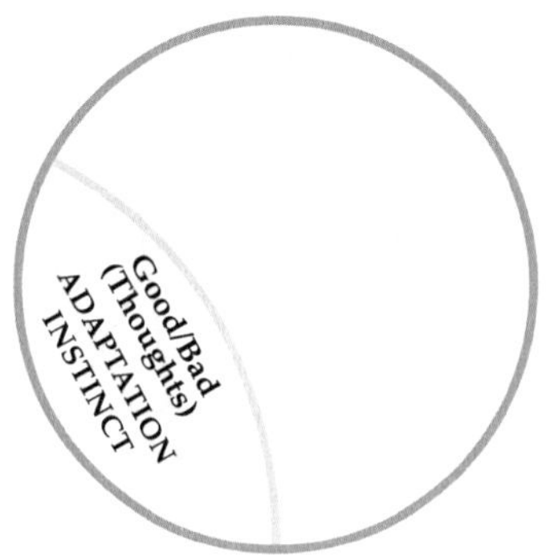

THE ADAPTATION INSTINCT

Following the second Law of Trialectics, the Law of Circulation, each one of these personas or egos has its own interest toward survival in its particular and distinct area of perception (physical, emotional and intellectual), which develops into a triad following this second Law of Circulation where, because of the internal activities of any monad or unity, a process of circulation is produced where first the monad appears as the *result* or being in repose, second as the *action,* and finally as the *reaction.*

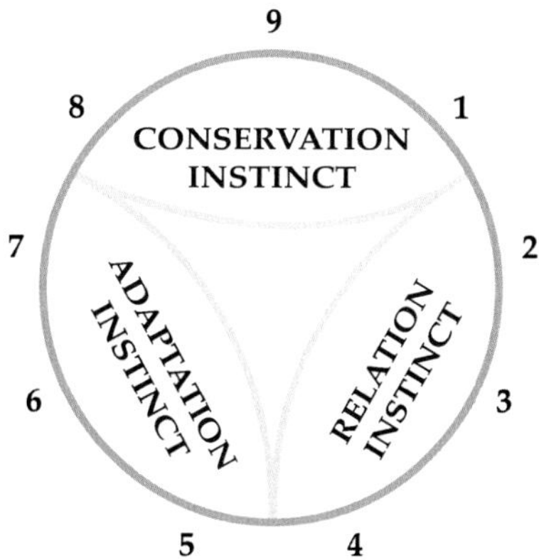

ENNEAGRAM OF THE THREE INSTINCTS

Because the three Instincts function in an intimate relationship and constantly depend on each other, as happens with the Poles, they become integrated as three triads, forming an ennead that can be inscribed in an enneagram. Now the triad of Instincts relating to our physical, emotional and intellectual life becomes intimately interrelated by the dynamic movement of the Unity, or what in Trialectics is known as the "function," which is the purpose of survival or the manifestation of the 'will to live' in the three interrelated aspects of physical–conservation, emotional–social relationships, and intellectual–adaptation to the natural and cultural environment, for our own benefit. As pointed out, the three Instincts manifest as three different entities or egos, each with its own level of manifestation and with its own particular way of perceiving reality by a teleological finality as its own dynamic. Thus, the physical Conservation Instinct perceives through the sensations (Feelings) of the viscera and, in general, interprets its own reality in terms of like or dislike, or of taking or repulsing any given element in accordance with the survival principle that is the foundation of this Instinct.

The emotional Relation Instinct perceives its reality in terms of love or hate and, in general, emotional attachment or aversion. The intellectual Adaptation Instinct perceives its own intellectual reality in terms of truth and falsity or right and wrong. Consequently, these three instinctual personas or egos, with their internal dynamics of the Law of Circulation, will produce in each Instinct three different aspects or ego–positions, and therefore, three different perspectives of reality. The three Instincts develop an ennead of aspects between them that can be inscribed in an enneagram. Thus, we have nine ego–positions, three for each Instinct, at the level of the Existential Mind (Sphere 15), and these three triads of Instincts are always manifested simultaneously, since the manifestations of the intellectual, emotional and somatic–physical aspects of our psychic life have to be present at the same time and in close interdependence as a triad. These nine aspects of perceiving reality or, more concretely, the three instinctual points of view and modes of perceiving reality become developed in succession during infancy and childhood by our Instincts encountering and interrelating with our parents—the mother, the conservation aspect; the father, the social relation aspect; and the intellectual, adaptation aspect by relating to our environment across our siblings, peers, playmates, and the world.

Besides these three different instinctual influences that form the actual particular point of view of each ego, each with an inclination toward adapting to one of three alternatives, the

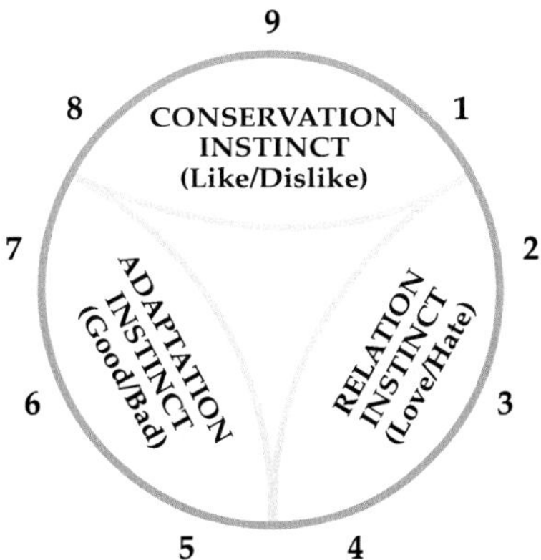

ENNEAGRAM OF INSTINCTUAL PERCEPTIONS

egos also receive the influence of the Primordial Mind (Sphere 16) and the structure of the Sexual Pole. The gender and sexual inclination have already been formed in the intrauterine environment prior to birth, and the Spiritual Pole is formed at the time of birth and during the first two weeks of life, where the infant feels whether they have come into a world that is warm, loving, benevolent, and good or into a world that is cold, unloving, malignant, and bad. Thus, the primordial attitudes of gender and faith will be decisive for the perception that will fixate the attention of a given ego and immobilize it into a hardened ego–position of attention with a narrow or partial point of view.

Now the Existential Attitudes will be defined and will become the background of the three different ego–positions of each triad that each ego may fall into because of an increasing awareness of one of these three ego–positions. If a particular ego threatens you by affecting your survival because it is failing and weak, the ego–position becomes fixated by this threat and further on, atrophied and hardened. Because of the primordial

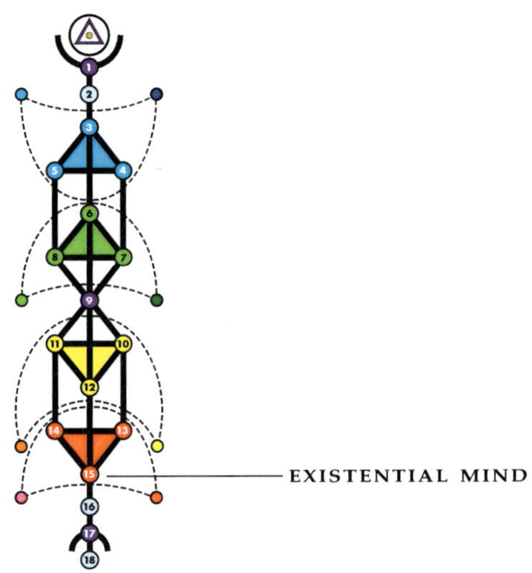

manifestations of the two main Polar Preconceptions, first the sexual attitude of gender and sexual inclination appears and manifests as the way of attracting and winning a partner; and second, sexuality appears in the sense of procreation and survival of the species, as in the Darwinian formulation of the 'Law of the Survival of the Fittest.' The Spiritual Pole manifests as the conquering and defense of the two most distinct human aspirations: the acquiring of power by way of war or political ambition, and the attainment of mystical spirituality by way of philosophy, religion and the sciences.

When these Polar Preconceptions interrelate with the three main Existential Attitudes produced by the Instincts, there appears an innate set of Divine Forms—the Universal Transpersonal and Cosmic manifestations of the most basic aspects of our individuality. When one of the nine Divine Forms receives an overdose of internal pressure and aggressive psychic charge, it becomes void or absent, and this

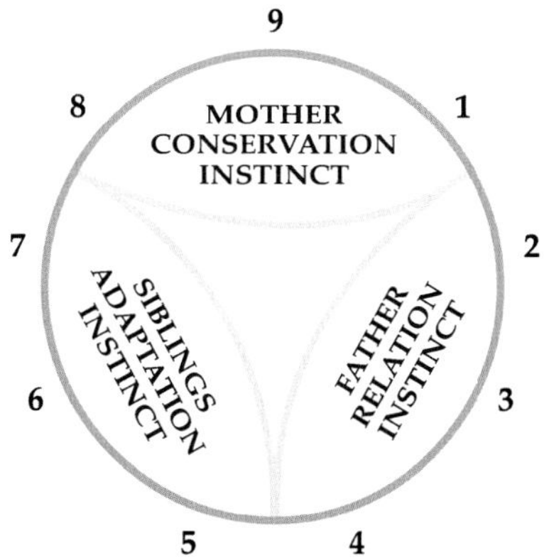

INSTINCTUAL POINTS OF VIEW

absence of the Divine Forms makes the ability and function of reproducing the Divine Light untenable. Instead, in the void produced by this absence, lack or loss, there develops an Ego–Fixation in its partial and narrow ego–position, which is now actually substituting for the Universal and transcendent lost Divine Form. Then what we have is a set of nine ego–positions with nine obscurations or distorted views of reality in the absence of the Universal corresponding Divine Forms. These nine ego–positions view everything from the perspective of the complete subjectivity, peculiarity and private point of view of the Ego–Fixation. The Existential Mind (Sphere 15), where the Ego–Fixations occur, is composed of three Instincts with their corresponding three instinctual subjects of Conservation, Relation and Adaptation. With the attendant sense of attention of three egos, this means that by necessity there will be three fixed points, each one corresponding to one of the instinctual egos. Because of this, there will also be the lack or the loss of three Divine Forms. This fixated triad in Protoanalytic terminology, a "Trifix," becomes pivotal for the structure of the entire psyche.

ENNEAGRAM OF THE FIXATIONS AND THE DIVINE FORMS

The nine ego–positions show nine effects or particular points of view that are in reality obscurations of the corresponding nine Divine Forms, and consequently there are nine distorted and erroneous points of view that do not fit with reality, which can be perceived only across the clarity of the nine Divine Forms.

This is to say that the clarity of the nine Divine Forms gives us the direct perception of transcendentality and of what in the Integral Philosophical Theory is known as Objective Reality, reality as it is perceived by a Mind activated by one of the Divine Forms or the sum of all of them. The Divine Forms are then reflections of the Transcendental Divine Mind of God.

This Mind of Transcendentality, the seventh Sphere in the scale of The Scarab, is termed the Creative Mind or the Mind of God in the creative process. Here the Divine Forms are the

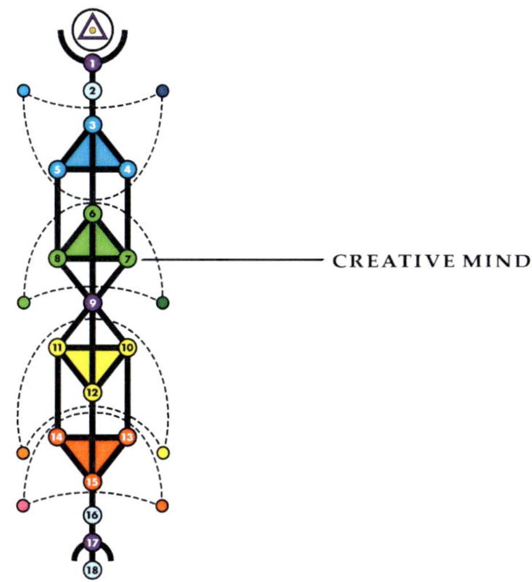

actual Forms (or Ideas) in the strictest Platonic sense —the Forms that God reveals in Objective Reality and upon which the entire material world is suspended, created and manifested. But when the three basic Instincts become fixated in the Trifix, and when the loss of the three Divine Forms becomes operative, the Trifix develops its own peculiar, particular, personal, and narrow point of view.

In this way, the world of the Trifix, or the composite of the three Ego–Fixations that develop into three egos, will color the entire outlook of the person, making it entirely subjective and particular because of the loss of the three Divine Forms. An excessive attention that fixates the entire psyche upon the demands of the completely subjective, distinct and personal points of view of the Trifix has replaced the now obstructed Universal points of view of the Divine Forms.

Pherecydes was the first pre–Socratic philosopher who spoke about the existence of two contradictory points of view—one

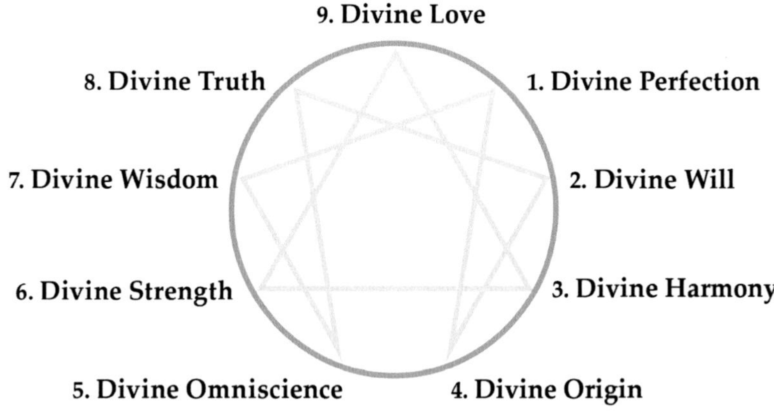

ENNEAGRAM OF THE DIVINE FORMS

subjective and personal and the other objective and Universal. Pythagoras gives us the same division, leaving the ego–position of subjectivity to the unenlightened mind and defining the Superior Enlightened Mind by way of the first nine digital numbers or philosophical numbers of his system. Heraclitus gives us an even more strict definition of the subjective and the objective ego–positions, in which he qualifies the former as a mind that is asleep and that creates its personal, private world with no real communication with the outside social environment, and the latter as a Mind that is awakened to Objective Reality, the Transcendental Reality of what is Universal, and consequently lives not in a subjective, private, obscure, and narrow world, but is awakened into the Light of the Universal, common world, where intercommunication exists because of the common Objective and Divine Fire that permeates both our common Universe and our common humanity. Parmenides, in his magnificent philosophical poem *On Nature,* gives us the difference between the two ways by defining what belongs to "The Way of Truth" as unchanging and Universal, while "The Way of Opinion" is one of change and multiplicity. By showing the axiomatic logical principles of identity, contradiction and the excluded middle, Parmenides became the founder of the Principles of Formal Logic, which was duly employed by Aristotle in his *Posterior Analytics*. In Plato's *Philebus*, Socrates presents the same double standard, one that corresponds to the True Self which is Universal, and the other that corresponds to the personal ego and its collection of obscure and mixed opinions. The founder of Stoicism, Zeno of Citium, as well as the great Stoic systematizers, Chrysippus and Cleanthes, who were admitted followers of Heraclitus, expanded the definitions as well as the phenomenology of the Heraclitean asleep and awakened states of mind, the former belonging to the ego–personality and the latter to the True Self. Among the Neoplatonists, the discussion of the Mind of Unity and the Mind of Plurality is exhaustively examined by Proclus in his *Elements of Theology*. We can see this same division in the Renaissance philosophers Ficino, Pico and Bruno; and in modern times in Leibniz, Kant, Lotze, Brentano, and their followers. This division—which is especially structured in human language and culture—of a superior and pure intellectual mind and an inferior mind, is the main thematic of contemporary phenomenology, linguistics, positive analysis, existentialism, and deconstruction.

In the Integral Theory, the two Minds are described in their structure, and defined in the series of The Scarab—each one of the Minds being composed of nine Spheres or levels of perception of reality. Each Sphere itself is analyzed in the geometric figure of an enneagram showing the circularity of the dynamics of the ennead.

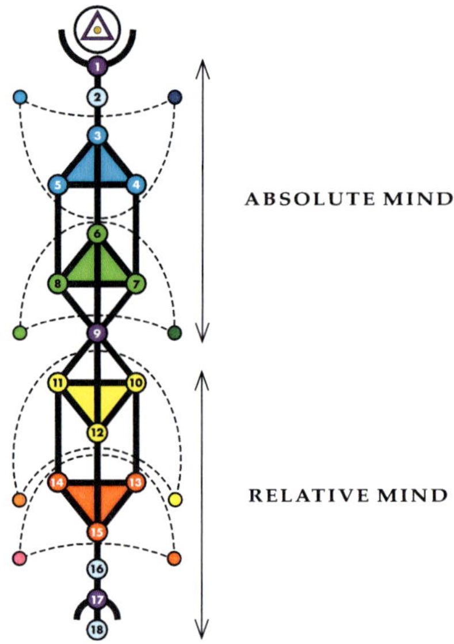

Further on, the Spheres are inscribed in an enneagram where we can study the logical interrelations between the nine points. The nine Spheres that correspond to the Superior Mind or, in Integral terms, to the Absolute Mind, are numbered 9 to 1 in The Scarab. The Inferior Mind, which in Integral terms is known as the Relative Mind, is numbered by the series in The Scarab from 18 to 10. The strict difference between the Relative Mind of the inferior ego and the Absolute Mind of the Superior Divine Self is that the Absolute Mind is transcendental in all its nine Spheres. This is to say that these Spheres can only be discovered and disclosed by way of a Mind of Transcendentality that as such necessarily abides in total quietude, serenity and peace, as well as in the clarity and transparency of a Mind that is pointing at itself in a profound Self–remembering of the Pure Nature of the Absolute Mind as being the union of the

Calm–abiding Quietude of Mind, a Mind that has entered into a State of *Ataraxia* (Gk), which is without any mental movement—just staying or abiding in the natural Mind without thoughts. By entering into a Mind of *Epoche* (Gk), or the cancellation of the analytical processes of the multiple and plural discriminative judgment of the Relative Mind of Concepts and Language, the Natural Mind arises.

By definition, when we experience through any Sphere of the Absolute Mind the perception of reality as being transcendental and in a state of perfect neutrality without thoughts or desires, we enter into a general State of *Apatheia* (Gk), giving up all attachments, bad habits, and subjective emotions. In direct correspondence, the Relative Mind, with its nine Spheres of relative thought and perception (Spheres 18–10), when not discovered and disclosed by methodic analysis of its structure and the link of causation or prior antecedence between these Spheres, becomes the structure of the lower ego with its nine Spheres of distorted reality, which become manifested at different levels in each one of them. The first Spheres of The Scarab are those we have analyzed up to here: the Somatic Mind (Sphere 18), the Cognitive Mind (Sphere 17), the Primordial Mind (Sphere 16), and the Existential Mind (Sphere 15). It is in this last mind that the ego forms its main basic structure shown in the Enneagram of the Three Instincts, which develops into the Enneagram of the Ego–Fixations and the attendant Passions.

Following the Integral Theory, the correspondent Sphere to the Existential Mind (Sphere 15) in the set of nine Spheres of the Absolute Mind is the Creative Mind (Sphere 7). As we advance, the Creative Mind expresses itself in a set of nine Divine Forms shown inscribed in an enneagram (see page 26) in Integral Philosophy.

ENNEAGRAM OF THE EGO–FIXATIONS AND PASSIONS

The basis of nine is found in the Philosophical Numbers of the Pythagorean system, which was based upon the existence of nine heavenly bodies. In Platonic theology the Pure Ideas of the Mind of Superior Intellect are the Supreme Patterns of all Creation, though Plato never actually described them or numbered them. In fact, the Divine Ideas (Forms) are the transcendental Absolute point of view from the side of Total Reality or God. This, of course, is contrasted with the nine obscure and distorted points of view presented in the Enneagram of the Ego–Fixations in the Sphere of the Existential Mind (Sphere 15). Remember that the Ego–Fixation is a hardened point of attention, preoccupation and care in which we are extremely sensitive because of the distortion produced by the absence

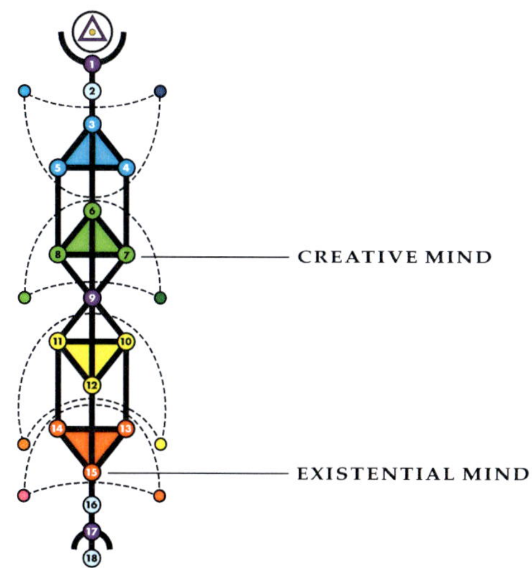

of the corresponding Divine Form. Therefore, we have to conclude that to restore the balance of the lost Divine Forms, we have a double task to accomplish.

First, it is necessary to dissolve the hardening of the Ego–Fixations by way of observation, recognition and *Katharsis* (Gk), or the thorough purification of all the stagnant elements in the Trifix. Second, by way of entering into the Absolute Mind and with the help of the Primordial Light that is to be found in the ninth Sphere of The Scarab, it is possible to open and disclose with transcendental, intuitive insight the content and nature of the Divine Forms. In other words, it is necessary to produce the Mind of Transcendentality of the ninth Sphere, which in The Scarab is called the "Enlightened Mind."

The Enlightened Mind (Sphere 9) is the Mind of Unity that harmonizes the nine lower spheres of the Relative Mind with the nine superior Spheres of the Absolute Mind. The Enlightened Mind is at the very center of the schema of The Scarab and

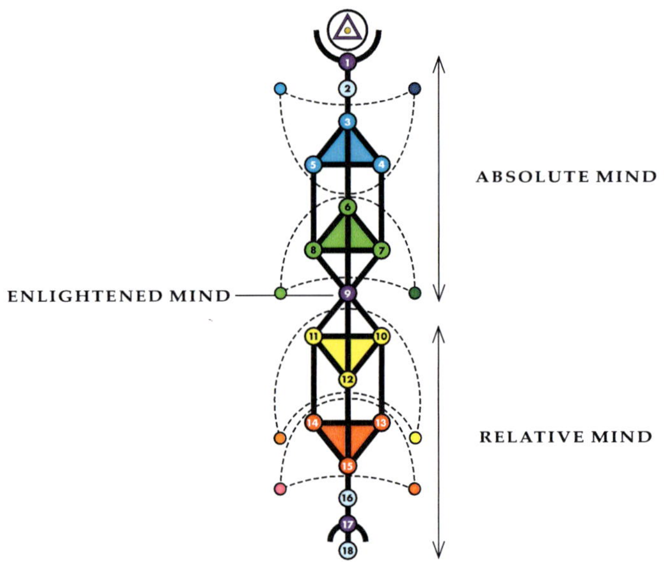

unifies the otherwise separate realms of the Relative and the Absolute Minds. Once a Mind of Transcendentality is attained by the Unity of the Relative and the Absolute Minds, then there appears the internal 'arc of Unity,' the recognition that the content of the mind or its own thoughts, and the mind itself as the source of these thoughts, are one and the same. The 'arc of Unity' instantly ignites a profound insight and Innate Awareness, a point of view that changes all other points of view, with a way to see reality without the disturbance of the subjective mind, which is transcended by the recognition that, in fact, "All is Mind."

With the power of the Enlightened Mind of Unity, it is possible to experience the eighth Sphere, known in the scheme of The Scarab as the Volitional Mind, whose content is shown in Integral Philosophy in the Enneagram of the Divine Energies. The Divine Energies are the actual internal teleological

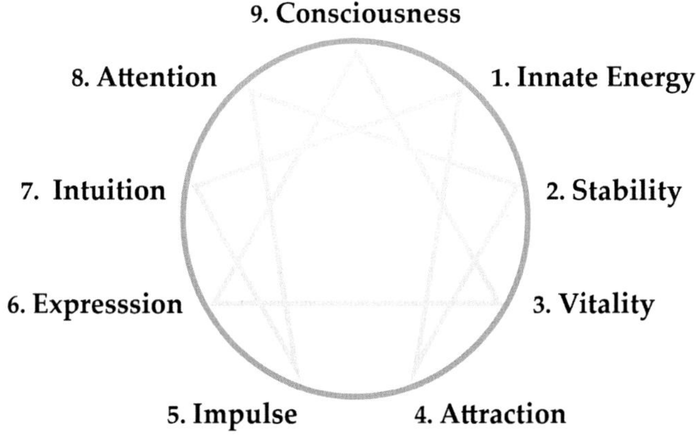

ENNEAGRAM OF THE ENERGIES

motivation and/or purpose toward realization of the Divine Forms. Through the Divine Energies, we can enter into the seventh Sphere, the Creative Mind, the content of which is the nine Divine Forms. The 'Creative Mind in itself' equates to the Platonic Forms or Ideas. Thus, the 'Creative Mind in itself' is the Intellectual Principle, the Idea of the 'Universe as such,' or the Universe as Ultimate Reality.

The nine Divine Forms are the nine possible Forms in which the Intellectual Principle can be realized. Thus, there is a Unity and a hierarchy between the Divine Forms. If we truly acquire one, we acquire the other eight since they are innate aspects of the One Totality that is the Intellectual Principle. Then, the Creative Mind can be said to have as its content two elements—the Intellectual Principle and the nine Divine Forms. Thus, the Intellectual Principle is the base, the foundation, or the ground of the Creative Mind, and the nine Divine Forms are the energy of the Intellectual Principle or the ground of the Creative Mind manifested in nine Divine Forms. Together the nine Divine Forms have to be understood as Essential and Universal Forms, and consequently it can be said that they are the Universal Concepts of God. This is to say that they are the thoughts and thought of God in a strict Platonic sense. Therefore, the Forms cannot be subjective or belonging to somebody's individual intellection, because the Divine Forms are Universal concepts. Because of this, they do not belong to the Trifix realm of the ego, and when the Divine Forms are disclosed in the Creative Mind (Sphere 7), the subjectivity of the Trifix collapses and the hardened Ego–Fixations dissolve into the open and Universal Energy of the Divine Forms.

We have to observe that the 'Intellectual Principle in itself' is the nine Divine Forms. This is to say that the nine Divine Forms are the reflection of the Intellectual Principle. Thus, they are one and the same, and they are completely inseparable, since one means the other, and we can find a logical separation only when thought as a whole becomes divided into the ego–positions of the Knower, the Intellectual Principle, and the Known, the Divine Forms. But we have to insist that the difference is only logical since, at the level of Transcendence beyond the ninth Sphere of the Enlightened Mind, the Known and the Knower are united into Transcendentality and Oneness in all the Spheres of the Absolute Mind (Spheres 9–1).

The nine Divine Forms of the Creative Mind are the Mind of God, God in His mode of Supreme Intellectual Principle or Supreme Creator, who thinks and by thinking creates the Universe. The Primordial Creation in the Mind of God is the Ultimate Reality of the Universe, the Universe as it really is.

The Divine Forms, when manifested in the material realm at the level of the Existential Mind (Sphere 15), where we find the three Instincts and their nine possible Ego–Fixations, project the intense force of the Forms as Models of Perfection that dissolve and annihilate the engrossing stagnation of the Trifix. Thus, we can say that under the influence of the Divine Forms, which in Integral Philosophy are also called the "Psychocatalyzers," a process of transcending the habitual patterns of behavior produced by the Trifix is possible. The Divine Creation manifests by means of emanation from the Divine Forms down into the material reality of the Ego–Fixations. By the impulse of returning that manifests as an attraction toward the Divine Forms, they act as a progressive ladder that rises from the temporal Ego–Fixations or the ego's points of view, which are now transformed teleologically or purposefully into the Eternal Divine Forms. This progressive realization of the Divine Forms means that there is a teleological cosmic plan, a cosmic purpose, and a Universal motivation that proceeds in accordance with a plan of progressive perfection and realization of the pure Immortal Ideas of the Divine Forms.

Integral Philosophy asserts that the Divine Forms, because they themselves are Eternal and unchangeable, while in the process of transcending the Trifix (the triple Ego–Fixation), do not become part of the process of transformation from a fixated point of view to a liberated and open point of view. But they act in a way similar to chemical elements that perform as catalyzers, in which the catalyzer provokes a chemical reaction without being changed.

In this way, the Divine Forms catalyze the process of dis-

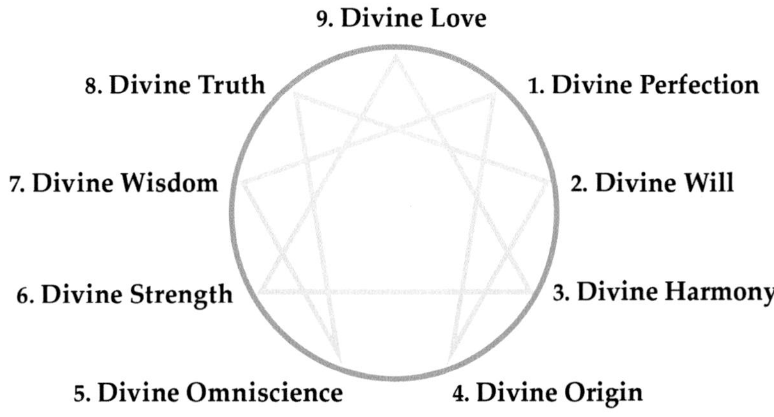

ENNEAGRAM OF THE DIVINE FORMS

solving the Ego–Fixations without any change to themselves. For this reason in Integral Philosophy they are characterized as "Psychocatalyzers," whose outcome is freedom from the fixated ego–position. When the fixated ego–positions disappear, our psyche returns to its own natural, primordial condition that was there before the triple Ego–Fixation occurred. This return to the natural state is called the "Divine Child" by the Orphic and Pythagorean Mysteries (sixth century BC) or the "embryo" by the Taoist tantrics (second century AD). The reference is to the state of innocence, because the Mind now functions through the Divine Forms with an open view into Reality as it is, without the prejudices of obscurations and preconceptions of the fixated ego–position. This new perspective granted by the Divine Forms is the point of view of the Enlightened Mind. Thus, we have nine different ways to see God in theological terms, and consequently nine Universal Ways we can experience Ultimate Reality. To experience a Divine Form is to experience an understanding of what is unchanging, Eternal and stable. In this way, we can really transfer our point of view from the Ego–Fixation into the Essence of a Divine Form.

By a systematic approach to the Divine Forms, we can awaken a consciousness that is capable of transcending the hardness of the Ego–Fixation; this must be apprehended by a devout emotion and actually shaken by a religious awe in the face of Eternity. This solemn approach to the Divine Truth is steered by an intuition of the One Creator of all living beings. This monotheistic perspective results in strong emotions of brotherhood and kinship with all that is our common creation, and our ego–boundaries and misconceptions become transcended. The radiating love that is at the top of the Enneagram of the Divine Forms will permeate our entire being and produce an intense Divine Love that will perceive God in everything.

This process of working with the Psychocatalyzers recovers the purity of the Creative Mind by dissolving the Ego–Fixations of the Existential Mind, which is composed of the three Instincts (Conservation, Relation and Adaptation) which, when liberated, will naturally and spontaneously reflect the Divine Forms. This is to say that the Divine Forms will function by reacting objectively in accordance with what the Instincts demand from us: our sense of the Conservation Instinct involving all our physical preservation; our Relation Instinct with all its ability for social communication and interaction; and our Adaptation Instinct which gives a true perspective for working appropriately with our natural and social environment. Once the Instincts are recovered from the influence of the Existential Attitudes of Sadness and Depression (Conservation), Anger and Anxiety (Relation), and Fear and Stress (Adaptation), they function

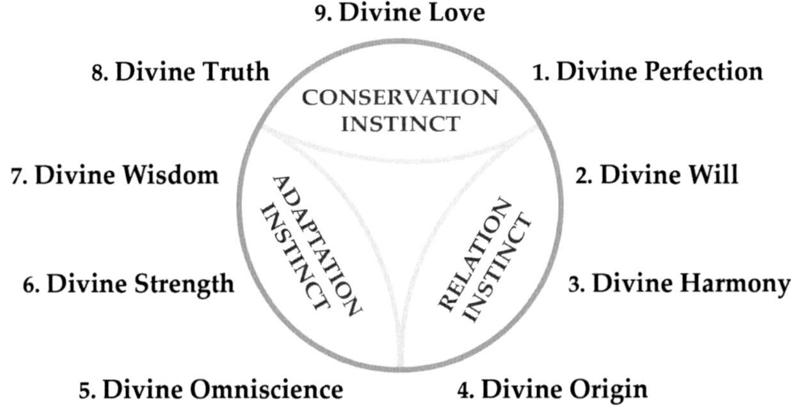

ENNEAGRAM OF THE DIVINE FORMS AND THE THREE INSTINCTS

as a harmonic and co–dependent triad, without the internal contradictions produced by the radical differences of the particular interests of each Instinct.

When the Instincts have been liberated from their subjective manifestations of the Existential Attitudes, they will influence the Primordial Mind (Sphere 16) where we find the two Poles of Sex and Spirit which had altered their natural function by denying the innate flow of the Spiritual Drive toward Knowledge, understanding and union with the world. Instead, the Spiritual Pole had been interiorized and had obtained a misdirected outcome through the Sexual Pole, manifesting in the form of an aggressive vitality that makes war from the very beginning. And the outcome of this imbalance is the ferocity and hate toward a world that has to be conquered, tamed and subdued. This general aggressivity is known as the "Polar Preconception" in Integral Philosophy. When the Instincts have been liberated from their Existential Attitudes, the Polar Preconception will start to dissolve, but to complete this

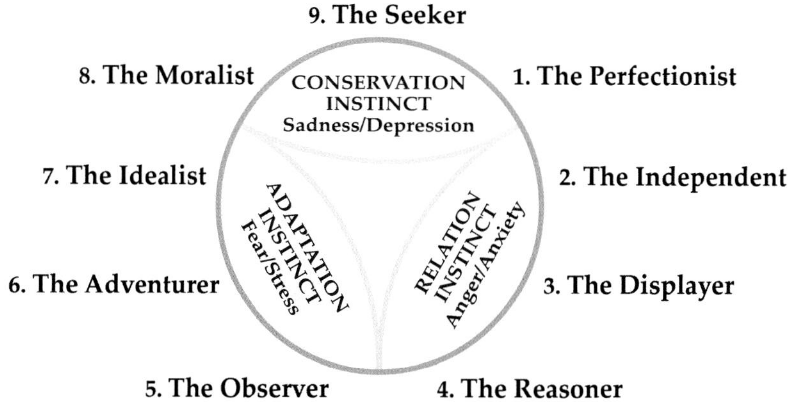

ENNEAGRAM OF THE FIXATIONS, INSTINCTS AND EXISTENTIAL ATTITUDES

return to the natural state—in which the Sexual Pole implies a free, happy and healthy vitality, and the Spiritual Pole flows toward the Union with what is spiritual and belongs to The Good, The One, and The Eternal—it is necessary to awaken the Illuminative Mind, Sphere 6 in the scheme of The Scarab, whose content is the Enneagram of the Integral Virtues.

In Integral Philosophy, the content of the Eighteen Spheres of Existence, Knowledge and Immortality is described in terms of enneagrams, figures that describe cyclical processes of the psyche. A cyclical process is characterized by the three Laws of Trialectical logic. The first Law, the Law of Mutation, establishes the hierarchical manifestation of anything in reality, or the nine steps of any process which develops in a cyclical way, where the last aspect of the process is connected to the first as in, for example, the spectrum of the colors of light. This Law is represented by the outside circle of the enneagram, with points numbered one to nine. The second Law of Trialectics, the Law of Circulation, establishes that the process is that of

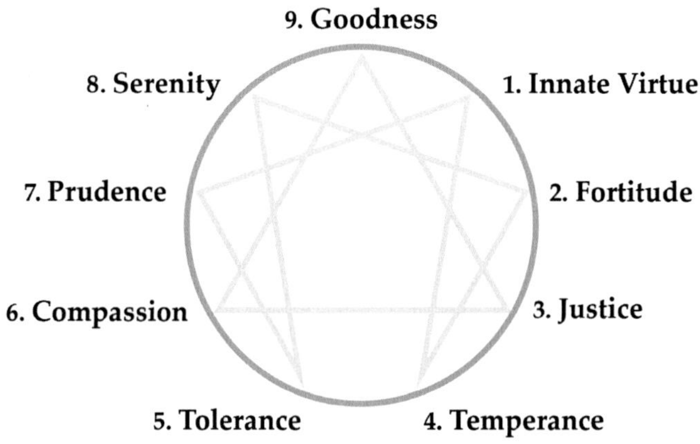

ENNEAGRAM OF THE INTEGRAL VIRTUES

becoming its opposite, like the process of hot (heat) becoming cold, wet becoming dry, night becoming day, or life becoming death. The process itself happens due to the triadic manifestation of the moments of the process in the triad first described by Plotinus, Porphyry, Iamblichus, and finally established by Proclus, who evokes the *Chaldean Oracles* as canonical revelation and authority, establishing that everything in the Universe manifests in triads.

This Law is applied to the enneagram by representing in the division of the enneagram figure the three Instincts and their related numbers, not on the basis of a hierarchical series, as in the case of the first Law, the Law of Mutation, but by the formation of three triads which complete one ennead or three sets of triads, implying the perfect motion of an internal cyclical process. This ennead is represented in the enneagram by dividing it into three sections: the upper part with the numbers 8, 9 and 1 (Conservation); the right side with the numbers 2, 3 and 4 (Relation); and the left side with the numbers 5, 6 and 7 (Adaptation).

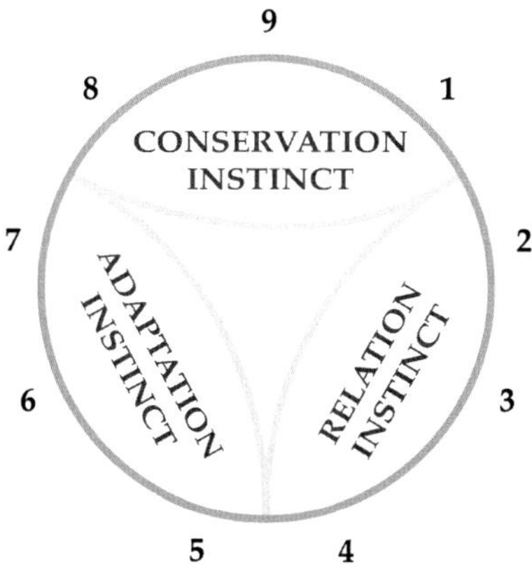

ENNEAGRAM OF THE THREE INSTINCTS

The fundamental function that the enneagram of triads represents is the interconnection and interdependence between the triads in order to produce a unitary reality or an actual process. In this way, in order to describe the content of the Enneagram of the Three Instincts, Sphere 15 of The Scarab, the three fundamental Instincts are a development of three main organic Systems whose actual function manifests in the three basic Instincts of Conservation or self–preservation, Relation in a societal community, and Adaptation of the environment to our needs. These three basic Instincts, because they are a triad, behave in their internal cycle in accordance with the second Law of Trialectics (Law of Circulation), and consequently they manifest only in accordance with that interrelation. At the same time, the three points or the triad of each Instinct has the internal motion that produces the precise Neoplatonic cyclic terms of proceeding, returning and sustaining, and in Trialectics as *action, reaction* and *result*. These three terms are supported by a teleological *function* or purpose of the motion itself which, in the triad of the Instincts for example, is to manifest the 'will to live' or the most basic sense of survival in three interdependent forms, the three different aspects or requirements for our survival that have to manifest together or not at all.

The Instincts are already influenced by the Polar Preconception of the Primordial Mind (Sphere 16), where we find the Sexual and Spiritual Poles, and which develops into the Existential Attitudes of the three Instincts.

The Conservation Instinct develops the Existential Attitude of the horror of death, and this is the origin of our existential sadness and depression. This is the lower manifestation of the Instinct. In its higher manifestation, the Existential Attitude becomes one of searching for real Being in a permanent Transcendental Self and in the search for immortality. The Relation Instinct develops the Existential Attitude of the terror of enslavement, which is the origin of our lower existential anger and anxiety. The higher Existential Attitude becomes the search for a realized Consciousness, where we find the real morality of The Good that can transform the anger and anxiety of the lower Existential Attitude. The Existential Attitude of the Adaptation Instinct is the fear of conflict, and this is the origin of our lower existential fear and stress. The higher side is the existential search for true Knowledge or Gnosis, where we find the State of 'Mind–only,' transforming the lower attitudes of fear and stress. Thus, the inner preoccupation or the function of the Conservation Instinct is the experience of and the search for Being; in Integral terms, this triad numbered 8, 9 and 1 is known as the Being Group. The great concern of this group is to become a person with all the attributes and

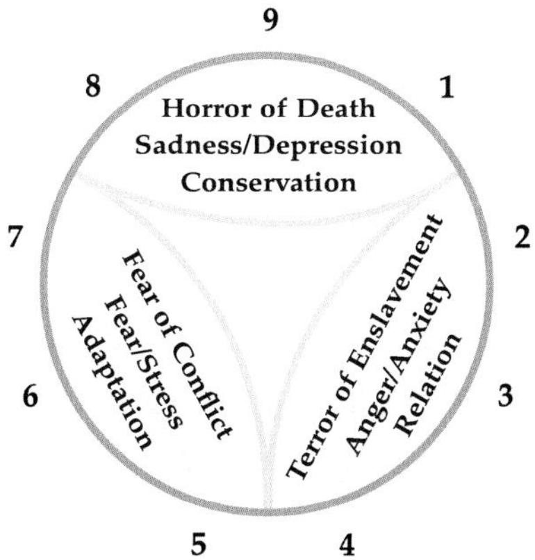

ENNEAGRAM OF THE EXISTENTIAL ATTITUDES

powers that are directly connected to our sense of God and immortality. This is to say, the problems of the Conservation Instinct, since they are related to the questions of the 'Being as such,' are ontological. The Relation Instinct triad, with the numbers 2, 3 and 4, is concerned with living in society, and is known as the Living Group. This Instinct cares about finding the Good Man and the higher moral, ethical person. Thus, the problems of the Relation Instinct are ethical. The Adaptation Instinct triad is composed of the numbers 5, 6 and 7, and this Instinct is preoccupied with adapting to the environment and doing what is necessary to control it. It is known as the Doing Group. This Instinct is interested in true Knowledge or Gnosis and Divine Providence manifested in the world. The problems of the Adaptation Instinct are metaphysical and concerned with Ultimate Reality.

In this way, Integral Philosophy observes that in the potential, or in what is innate to the Instincts, are the Divine Forms derived from the main triad that divides all reality into God or

Being, society or the 'good life,' and the world and its perfect Gnosis. At this point, the first enneagram developed from the triad of Instincts is the set of the Ego–Fixations or ego–positions, which replace and obscure the universality of the Divine Forms with the particular, subjective and fixated point of view of the Ego–Fixations. The Ego–Fixations in Protoanalysis are: (1) The Perfectionist, (2) The Independent, (3) The Displayer, (4) The Reasoner, (5) The Observer, (6) The Adventurer, (7) The Idealist, (8) The Moralist, and (9) The Seeker.

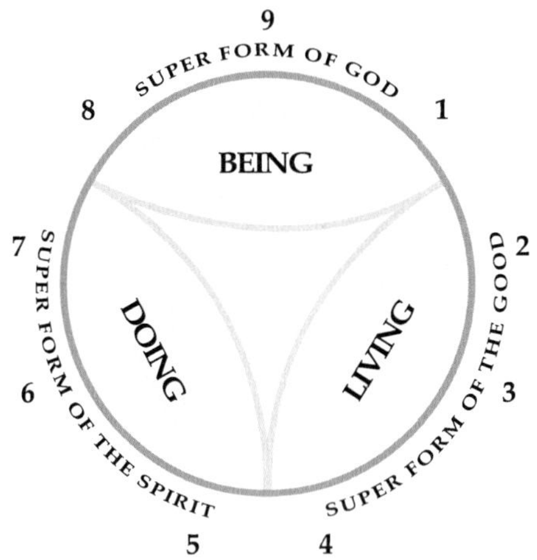

TRIAD OF THE SUPER FORMS

Because of the narrow and distorted point of view of the Ego–Fixations, a parallel enneagram develops on the emotional level, known as the Enneagram of the Passions. The Passions can be characterized as overloaded Ego–Fixations that are compensating for the narrow ego–position of the corresponding Ego–Fixation. The Passions are: (1) Anger, (2) Pride, (3) Deceit, (4) Envy, (5) Avarice, (6) Fear, (7) Gluttony, (8) Excess, and (9) Laziness.

The Passions are like analgesics to nullify the pain produced

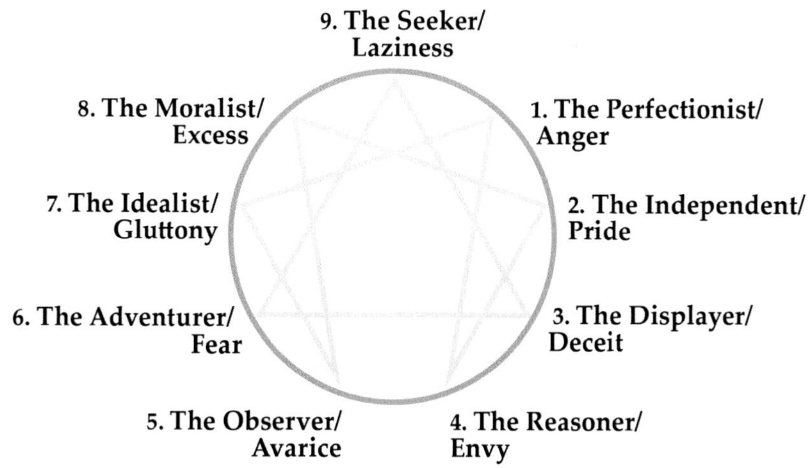

ENNEAGRAM OF THE EGO–FIXATIONS AND PASSIONS

by the absence of the Divine Forms. Then, when we need to find the positive Existential Attitude in seeking the One God, the 'good life,' and the True Gnosis, there develop what are known in Integral Philosophy as the Traps, which are originally analyzed in the Existential Mind (Sphere 15) with the Fixations. Contrary to the Passions, which are lower manifestations, destructive and death–dealers, the Traps are higher manifestations, constructive and life–giving. They manifest in a purposeful mode as the liberated basic Spiritual Drive of the Spiritual Pole in Sphere 16 of the Primordial Mind. The Traps are: (1) Perfectionism, (2) Freedom, (3) Efficiency, (4) Authenticity, (5) Observation, (6) Security, (7) Idealism, (8) Morality, and (9) Seeking.

As we have seen before, when the Spiritual Drive becomes internalized by the rejection of the world, instead of directly seeking knowledge of the world, it uses the Sexual Pole to project itself into the world, but this time as a subjective force, giving the sexual energy a vicious content that makes the natural aggressivity of the Sexual Drive become empowered with violent, dark and misdirected desires that are projected in the Ego–Fixations and the Passions. Integral Philosophy defines the Ego–Fixation in two ways: first, it is the product of the lack of a Divine Form, and by this lack becomes an obscure, narrow and distorted point of view; and second, this distorted point of view in reality is the product of an excessive attention fixated in one point in an obsessive manner that creates a particular habit, thus becoming prone to repeating the habit indefinitely and becoming alienated further and further from the Pure Light of the Divine Form.

The excessive attention of the Ego–Fixation to its own point exclusively leads to a constant overdoing or an exaggeration of the point. As an example, Perfectionists (point 1) are obsessed with doing things perfectly and, even more, being perfect in themselves. When fixated in this point, this overdoing becomes obvious because the meticulousness and precision demanded by the Perfectionist becomes overdone, comical and grotesque. Curiously enough, all their close relationships will be aware of this obvious peculiarity of their character, but the Perfectionist will be totally unaware of it and will consider it a natural way to do and to be. It is this over–exaggeration of the Ego–Fixation that is the seed for the Trap of the Fixation.

The Trap here means the natural attraction of the Ego–Fixation toward the reward of finally becoming its obsession. In the case of the Perfectionist, for example, by searching for 'Perfection in itself,' in Protoanalytical terms

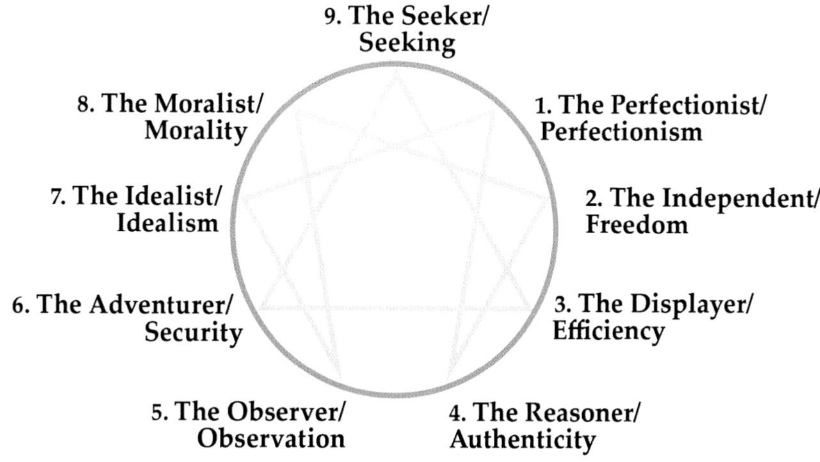

ENNEAGRAM OF THE EGO–FIXATIONS AND TRAPS

the Ego–Fixation becomes "trapped" in its own game. The Enneagram of the Traps is part of the content of the Theory of the Fixations of Sphere 15, the Existential Mind, and it belongs to the Volitional Mind (Sphere 8) of the Spheres of the Absolute Mind (Spheres 9–1 in The Scarab).

In the System of The Scarab in the ascending scale, the higher Sphere can only be opened by the preceding lower Sphere. Thus, theoretically speaking, to actually open the Traps, it is necessary to open the Enlightened Mind, Sphere 9 of The Scarab. The Enlightened Mind is exactly the middle point between the Spheres of the Absolute Mind (Spheres 9–1) and the Relative Mind (Spheres 18–10); it is the union between the Relative and Absolute Minds, since the totality of the Absolute Mind, with its nine Spheres, is the ground intellect of pure understanding and direct intuitive Knowledge. This is a Mind beyond the process of thinking or conceptualization and analytical

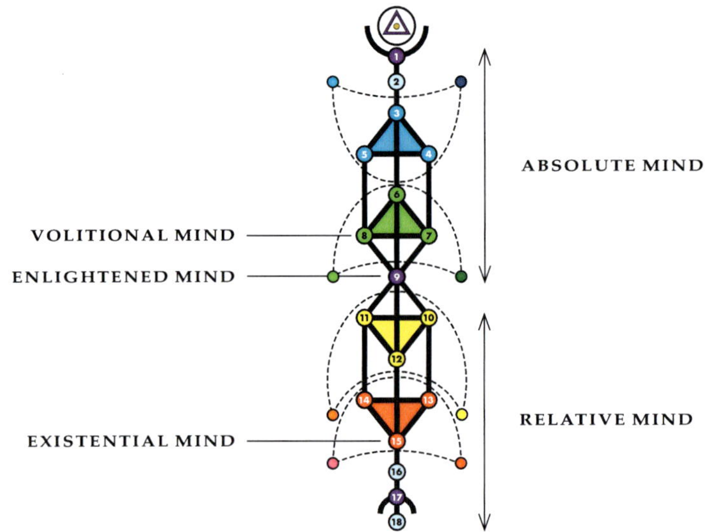

discrimination. This is a total Realm of Transcendentality, because it is beyond words in the sense that there are no material analogies with the ideas or the contents of the Absolute Mind. In the Sphere of the Enlightened Mind (Sphere 9), the Absolute Mind is viewed in its Totality, and it is found to be a Mind of Emptiness—empty of conceptualization, thinking and language.

But this Mind of Emptiness is indeed the ground for the Relative Mind (Spheres 18–10), seen here as a Totality that is nothing but the manifestation of the Pure Light. When the Relative Mind has been clarified—in the sense that the entire content of its own nine Spheres (Spheres 18–10) is nothing but Pure Light in diverse levels of relative manifestations—the same quality of being which is transitory, unstable and changing is totalized and presented as just Pure Light, empty of concepts. With this we come to realize that the thought process of the Relative Mind in reality equals the thought ground and transcendentality of the Absolute Mind. When, in the Sphere of the Enlightened Mind (Sphere 9), the Absolute and Relative Minds are disclosed as being empty of concepts and language, their inseparable Unity becomes realized; and by discovering the thought as ground or pure intellect, and the thinking process as the content or the intellection, the Unity of both is attained.

This Unity produces what, in Integral Philosophy, is known as the 'arc of Unity' or the union of the Relative and Absolute Minds, which attains an Ornamental Mind of the Transcendental State. Instantly, this Mind becomes Transcendental Pure Light. In this Mind of Unity, everything becomes the Light of Consciousness; in the Integral System, this is known as the "Birth of Light." It also signifies that the State of Enlightenment or the *epoche* of the Ancients is attained. This is a Mind of True Enlightenment in the sense that the Pure Light of Consciousness is now assimilated into a Mind of Transcendence that will manifest itself in the successive eight higher Spheres, thus maturing the Mind of Enlightenment into a total Mind of Divine Union or *Theosis* in the first Sphere—the Mind of Absolute Liberation from all 'Spheres of Knowledge' into the permanent and constant Innate Awareness of the Only One Divine in a State of Pure Light, Bliss, Joy, and Happiness in the fruition of the complete Total Mind. This Supreme Mind of *Theosis* means the restoration of the Divine Status of the Higher Self in humankind which is in us since the beginning of our life, has accompanied us throughout our life, and with which in its divinized State we will return to the Divine and Only One Source of what is Eternal, Infinite and unchangeable Pure Divine Light. Integral Philosophy asserts that the real destiny of humanity is to attain the real status of a divinized humanity, for all human beings equally have the Divine Spark of Light that we know as our True Innermost Self, which equally belongs to His Total Divine Perfection.

The actual Method of realizing the Mind of Unity in the Enlightened Mind (Sphere 9) is that of concentrating the attention on some point outside the body in space or on some point or points in the physical body, but even more specifically, in the points of energy in the central channel of the Subtle Body. The attention in these points is transformed into a state of deep concentration, while producing a deep relaxation in the body and letting the Mind settle in the State of Calm–abiding of its own Emptiness. This Mind of Emptiness is transformed into a Mind of Contemplation, in which the energies of the points in the central channel become transformed into an actual Divine Form, and the contemplation proceeds by way of vision of the 'Light in itself' and the understanding of the color that parallels or manifests as the Divine Form.

This way of seeing the Mind as Pure Light in its nine possible manifestations of the nine Divine Forms will attain for us an opening into the Pure Universality, Transcendentality and Immaterial Pure Light that exists only when the seventh Sphere of the Creative Mind with its nine Divine Forms is completely opened. Thus, it is necessary to insist that without a previous understanding of the Ego–Fixations of the Existential Mind (Sphere 15), and also the Unity of the Enlightened Mind (Sphere 9), the attainment of the Enlightened Mind is impossible. Sphere 7 of the Creative Mind has as its content the

Enneagram of the Divine Forms and, in the same way that the Ego–Fixations are the triadic manifestation of the three Instincts (Conservation, Relation and Adaptation), the Divine Forms are the reflection of the three most Universal Forms, represented by God and the 'Being as such,' man and the Absolute Good, and the Universe as Absolute Truth of Universal Light or Gnosis.

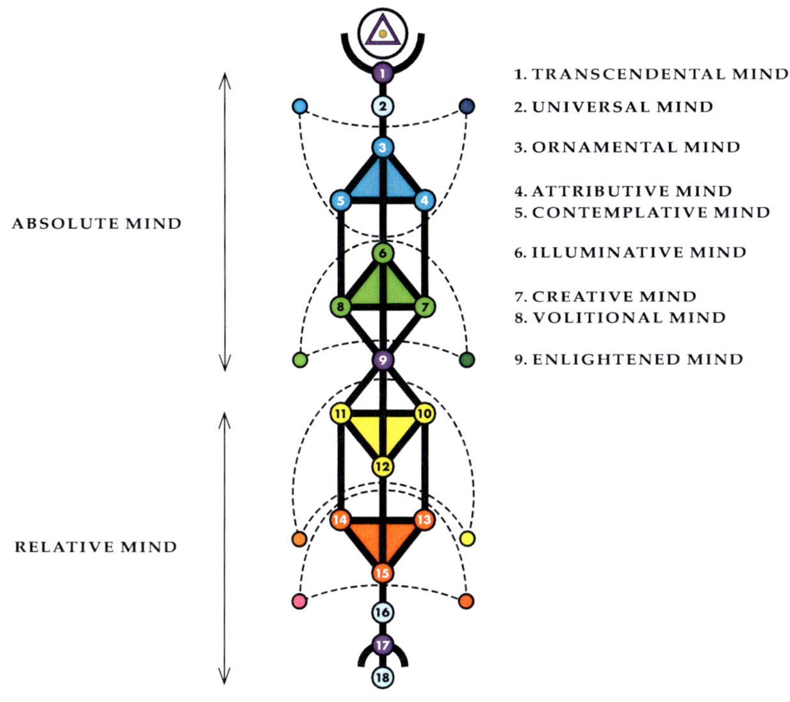

These three Super Forms become the ground of Totality and have to have by necessity a cause which in itself is not caused, what Aristotle called the unmoved mover or the First Cause. This is known as the cosmological proof of the existence of God. Aristotle explains that everything alive seems to follow a perfect pattern, as if everything behaves in accordance with the perfect design. Thus, it is a logical conclusion to realize the necessity of a Creator, and this points to the existence of God as a necessary designer or Creator of the Universe. Therefore, the Aristotelian Final Cause is the teleological necessity of a Divine Designer who provides perfect Laws for a perfect world. But the set of the four Aristotelian causes does not exhaust the investigation about the proofs of God, as Aristotle would have it, because the existence of God also has to be inferred from the fact that everything in reality is in relation to a certain degree with other things. This argument is developed by Plato in the *Republic*, who points out that we can always find a better good, but at the end we must come to imagine a Good that cannot be surpassed, a Good that is all the 'Goodness in itself.' This Good by necessity is God.

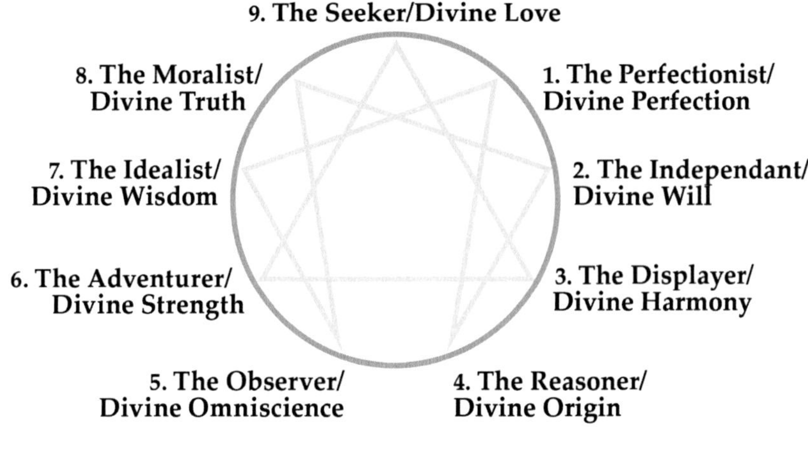

ENNEAGRAM OF THE FIXATIONS AND THE DIVINE FORMS

Thus, we can say that these classical proofs of the existence of God are the investigation of The Truth from five different perspectives: the first is the necessity of the existence of a foundational ground or Ultimate Reality, and this is the material proof; the second by necessity is the

Being equated with Pure Consciousness or Total Innate Awareness, Eternal and Unchangeable, giving the ontological proof; the third is the necessity of the immovable mover or that the Cosmos needs a cause—the cosmological proof; the fourth is the view from the perspective of the Laws that, though they transcend matter, they also organize it in harmonious sets of reality, proving by necessity the existence of the designer—the designer proof; and the fifth is that, when we observe that there is Good in the Universe, by necessity there has to be the Supreme Good (The Good) which attracts the entire Creation by way of an unstoppable desire in the form of love and compassion.

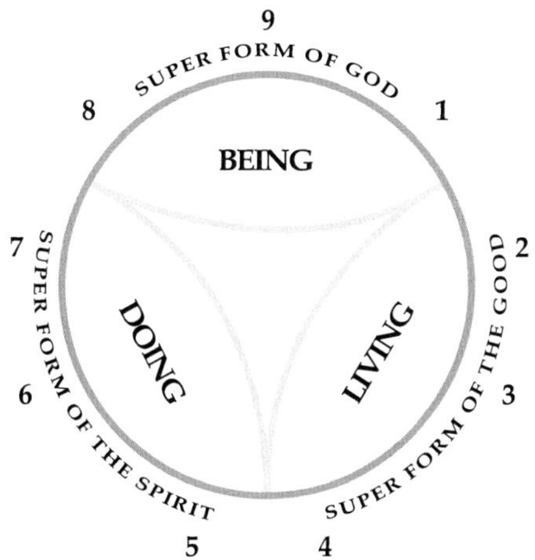

TRIAD OF THE SUPER FORMS

These proofs of the existence of God were appropriated by St. Augustine, St. Anselm, and St. Thomas Aquinas who quite naturally, with their sempiternal habits, did not give any reference to the very well–known sources of Plato, Aristotle, Posidonius, Plutarch, Numenius, and Plotinus. These are the five classical proofs for investigating the Form of Divine Truth. We have to be aware that they are only the proofs of the existence of God in their logical and intellectual understanding, and since the intellect cannot prove the Spirit adequately because by nature the Spirit and the spiritual are transcendental, in Integral terms the proofs belong exclusively to the Relative Mind. The 'Truth in itself' can only be found in the Absolute Mind in the set of the Divine Forms as Divine Truth. We can finally define Divine Truth as being the affirmation of the Existence of God, which is realized in the Total Innate Awareness of a Consciousness that has entered the Emptiness of Mind and sustains its purity without the obscuration of thinking and stays in the 'here and now,' thus actually entering into experiencing the cosmic Form of Divine Truth as the actuality of the Being that is found in the Perfect Innate Awareness of 'Consciousness in itself.'

The Enneagram of the Divine Forms is divided into three triads. The first triad, the Being Group, depends on the Super Form of God and the 'Being as such,' and this triad needs to be studied from the point of view of ontology, the study of the 'Being in itself.' This triad is composed of point 8, Divine Truth, as *action* (Neoplatonic "proceeding"); point 1, Divine Perfection, as the *reaction* ("returning"); and point 9, Divine Love, as the *result* ("sustaining"). The second triad, the Living Group, is based upon the Super Form of Man and the 'good life.' This triad has to be studied from the point of view of ethics or the Supreme Good, where point 2, Divine Will, is the *action* (proceeding); point 4, Divine Origin, is the *reaction* (returning); and point 3, Divine Harmony, is the *result* (sustaining). The third triad, the Doing Group, is based upon the Super Form of Universal Divine Wisdom, which is studied from the point of view of

ENNEAGRAM OF THE DIVINE FORMS, INSTINCTS AND SUPER FORMS

metaphysics, where point 5, Divine Omniscience, is the *action* (proceeding); point 7, Divine Wisdom, is the *reaction* (returning); and point 6, Divine Strength, is the *result* (sustaining).

The following material deals with the study of the Divine Forms or Psychocatalyzers in detail, as passed to the School in Arica, Chile in 1968. The material will then proceed with the study of the triads of God, Man and the Universe, following the sequence of their triadic manifestations of the *action* (proceeding), the *reaction* (returning) and the *result* (sustaining). Each Divine Form will be treated separately, following the schema of the Integral Mentational Analysis in the same way that it was presented in my lectures in 1969 at the Institute of Applied Psychology in Santiago, Chile; in 1970–71 in Arica, Chile; in 1972 in New York and San Francisco; in 1976 in the Kensho Lectures; in 1977 at the Shree Muktananda Ashram, South Fallsburg, New York; in 1978 at the *Cutting of the Adamantine Pyramid* training; in 1981 at Lincoln Center, New York; at Seabury Hall, Maui; and at the Collegiate Theatre, University of London, London, England; in 1982 at Maplecrest, New York and at the Wrekin Trust, Winchester, England; in 1990 at the Arica 22nd Anniversary Reunion, Kona, Hawaii; and in 1995 at the Arica 27th Anniversary Reunion, Maui, Hawaii.

	ARISTOTELIAN CAUSES	MENTATIONS	MENTATIONS QUESTIONS
ONTOLOGICAL	MATERIAL	SUBSTANCE	WHAT IS IT?
	FORMAL	FORM	HOW IS IT?
	EFFICIENT	POSSIBILITIES	WHY ORIGINATED?
	FINAL	NEEDS	WHAT PURPOSE?
ETHICAL	MATERIAL	IMPULSE	WHAT INTENTION?
	FORMAL	METHOD	HOW ACCOMPLISHED?
	EFFICIENT	STANDARD	WHAT IS THE IDEAL?
	FINAL	ORIENTATION	WHAT IS THE DIRECTION?
METAPHYSICAL	MATERIAL	CAPACITY	WHAT IS THE STRENGTH?
	FORMAL	CHARISMA	WHAT IS THE APPEARANCE?
	EFFICIENT	MEANS	HOW PRODUCED?
	FINAL	GOALS	WHAT IS ATTAINED?

The Mentational Analysis has been the basis for the presentation of the Divine Forms to the School since its beginning in Arica, Chile. The Mentational Analysis is a rhetorical schema of topics, an ordered sequence of questions to analyze and reveal the essential points of any given subject. This analysis differs from the classical rhetoric of Aristotle, Quintilian and Cicero, whose topics follow a logical sequence of a coherent series of questions that open and develop the understanding of a subject matter. Mentational Analysis is also a series of topical questions, but instead of following a logical presentation, it follows a metaphysical one on the basis of Aristotle's 'doctrine of causation' which we find in Book A of *Metaphysics*, where he presents his 'doctrine of the four causes' necessary for analyzing the metaphysical coherence of the 'doctrine of causation.' The causes are the material, the formal, the efficient, and the final. With these questions or topics of causation, Aristotle investigates the great metaphysical questions of being, knowledge and life. The series of the twelve Mentations reproduces the four Aristotelian causes, but each one is broken down three times in the Integral Analysis, which enlarges a further questioning of three of the causes in themselves—the formal, efficient and final. The material cause is the foundation of the entire subject matter and thus, is included in the three sets of topics. The first set of four analyzes from the point of view of ontology or the questions about the 'Being as such'; the second set of four analyzes from a position of ethics and values; and the third set of four analyzes from the perspective of metaphysical categories.

The following Divine Forms are also found in the published book of the Integral Theory, *Teachings of Integral Philosophy, The Nine Constituents, The Science of the Human Condition from Ego to Enlightenment*. The Divine Forms can be found in chapters about the Ego–Fixations in which each Fixation is presented from the origin of the Fixation to its highest point of manifestation. The fourteen–point Method of ego–reduction used in this presentation has been used in the Arica School since 1968.

CHAPTER 2

THE BEING GROUP

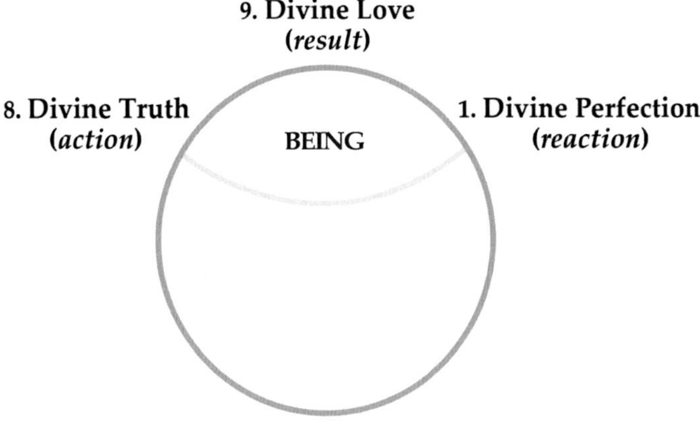

TRIAD OF THE BEING GROUP

In the triad of the Being Group, Divine Truth (point 8) is the point of *action* (proceeding) that is coming from the *result* (sustaining) point of Divine Love (point 9). Thus, it is an actual manifestation of Divine Love in the Form of Innate Awareness of the 'here and now.' The *action* (proceeding) of Divine Truth moves in the direction of the point of *reaction* (returning) of Divine Perfection (point 1). Thus, Divine Truth is the *action* point and Higher Presence capable of producing Transcendence or the Innate Awareness of the Divine. Therefore, Divine Truth means the affirmation of the existence of the One Divine God.

DIVINE TRUTH (Point 8)

The affirmation of the existence of God is the most fundamental Truth that human beings confront at the very beginning of their lives. In the moment that we confront our own being as existing and as being an alive creature, we face the question of there being a cause for this life that appears as a human being and disappears when death cuts life. Thus, the fundamental question of "What is our being?" has to be investigated by knowing what is the cause of our life as well as everything else in our environment. Therefore, we arrive at the even more fundamental questions of "What is the being in humans?" and "Is there a Transcendental Supreme Being who is God, the Creator of all?" Only the affirmative answer can be satisfactory to enter our human inner projection toward the Spirit as the most basic drive and force of the Spiritual Pole of the Primordial Mind (Sphere 16).

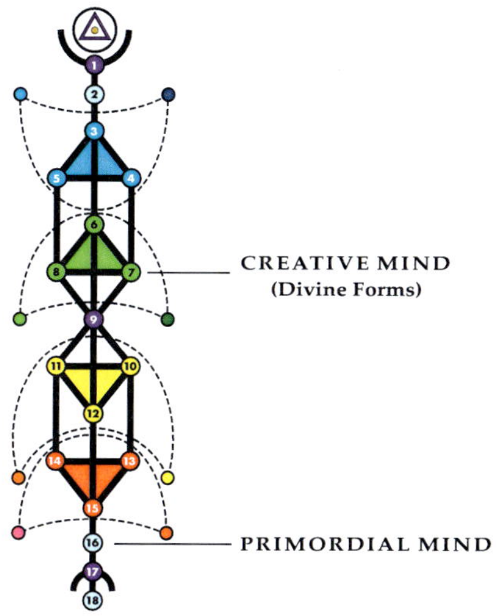

But to satisfy this primordial urgency in the psyche of human beings, it is necessary to prove the existence of God, as the first and most important question to be answered by philosophers, theologians and scientists. Aristotle calls this quite unmistakably the First Philosophy and he covers it in Book A of *Metaphysics*. In synthesis, he starts by pointing out that everything in the Universe depends on four causes—the material, the formal, the efficient, and the final. In the example of a chair, the material cause is the wood, the formal cause is the idea of the chair, the efficient cause is the carpenter who made the chair, and the final cause is that of being a chair for sitting. Aristotle then reminds us that the most fundamental question of the existence of God has only been answered by the philosophers in the first two causes, the material and the formal. The material cause was investigated by all the pre–Socratic philosophers, known as the Physicists, because they gave as an answer for the existence of God the necessity of an ultimate type of substance, a *physis* (Gk) which, by nature of being ultimate and thus, all–embracing, has to be simple and homogeneous.

This reminds us of the mysterious 'ultimate matter' of Spencer, and nowadays our most advanced cosmologists and physicists theorize about an ultimate stand of matter where, paradoxically, the matter becomes dematerialized into a substance without any attributes, known as 'singularity.' What is striking in this affirmation is that we can only be talking about pure space, which is the nature of consciousness. This, of course, is precisely the definition of the pre–Socratic Physicists for Ultimate Reality, which is transcendental, beyond matter, and absolutely simple and full of consciousness. Thales called it "water," which is a concept he took from the Egyptian priests, who called it "Nut," over which the eye of Ra floated—the Supreme Conscious Awareness united with the Transcendental Substance or the immaterial water. Anaximander called it the *Arche* (Gk) or pure, most simple mind stuff, ever–present, and unchangeable. Thus, for Aristotle, the Physicist philosophers were giving the answer to the question of God: He was the

Ultimate Substance in the Form of a Transcendental Reality and materiality, or a basic immateriality. Therefore, to term the Physicists as just materialists is missing the point, since their famous *physis* is commonly mistranslated as matter. In fact, it is something beyond matter for the very fact of its simplicity, homogeneousness and for being of the nature of consciousness. This misconception started with Aristotle himself who was famous for his belligerence about his predecessors. Thus, Aristotle indicated that the Physicist philosophers gave answers to the existence of God by discovering the substance of the Ultimate Reality. Therefore, the material cause is pointed out as the necessity of an Ultimate Transcendental Ground or Substance.

In the second proof for explaining the existence of God, Aristotle says that the formal cause or proof was the existence of 'being in itself,' or an Absolute Being that is defined as being immovable, unchanging and eternally one and the same always. This concept of 'Being as such' produces the logical Principle of Identity. Aristotle then points out that the formal cause for proving the existence of God was investigated by Parmenides and, because it is an investigation of the 'Being as such,' it is known as the ontological proof of God. In this analysis, Being is equated with Pure Thought or Pure Intellect in the sense of a Mind without concepts, empty of any thinking process. Thus, in the ontological proof, Being is found in Pure Innate Awareness.

Next, Aristotle analyzes the need to explain the origin of the Universe arguing that, since everything in reality has a cause, so does the 'Cosmos in itself,' as it transcends all and is the foundation of all Knowledge. The 'Cosmos in itself' is the base of the ontological proof of the existence of God, as we find in Aristotle, St. Anselm, and Descartes, who state that the awareness or consciousness of God and the existence of that consciousness are one and the same, or that our impression of the Truth of the Supreme Being and a State of Awareness of it are one and the same.

MENTATIONAL ANALYSIS OF DIVINE TRUTH

1 **SUBSTANCE** (What is it?) The substance of Divine Truth is the Innate Awareness of the 'here and now.' This means that the Truth of Being is permanent, immovable and unchanging. This is the Innate Awareness of what it is in itself, which is to say that the Truth or reality of a consciousness is that it has for its object the same consciousness. Consciousness looking at consciousness, like in a clear, untarnished mirror, is the Truth from which the nine Creative Ideas or Archetypal Forms manifest in the "Robe of Light" of the Gnostic Tradition.

2 **FORM** (How is it?) The Form or the Idea of Divine Truth is the sense of actual Eternity as the basis of the existence of the Divine.

3 **POSSIBILITIES** (Why originated?) The efficient cause of the 'here and now' of Divine Truth is manifested as Divine Presence or the Innate Awareness of the 'Being as such' as a Totality or a Divine Pleroma.

4 **NEEDS** (What purpose?) Divine Truth produces the Innate Awareness of the Pure Light of Transcendentality. This Pure Light is not in any sense material, but the actual manifestation of Transcendental Light of 'Con-

sciousness in itself.'

5 **IMPULSE** (What intention?) The innate impulse of Divine Truth is to dissipate the obscurations toward the Pure Light of Consciousness.

6 **METHOD** (How accomplished?) Divine Truth is accomplished by the Innate Awareness of the Divine or Pure Light.

7 **STANDARD** (What is the ideal?) The ideal of Divine Truth is the One God.

8 **ORIENTATION** (What is the direction?) The direction of Divine Truth is toward Eternity and Immortality.

9 **CAPACITY** (What is the strength?) The Transcendental Light of Divine Truth permeates and contains everything.

10 **CHARISMA** (What is the appearance?) Divine Truth presents itself to a Pure Consciousness in the form of the *Numinous,* or the internal Light that appears in a Mind of Quiescence and Non–conceptualization.

11 **MEANS** (How produced?) Divine Truth presents itself by means of its clarity, simplicity, uniformity, completeness, and Eternity.

12 **GOALS** (What is attained?) Divine Truth attains the contemplation of the Absolute Unity of God.

THE FIXATION OF THE MORALIST

Divine Truth has, in the correlative Enneagram of the Fixations of the Existential Mind (Sphere 15), the Ego–Fixation of the Moralist (point 8). Because this Ego–Fixation appears

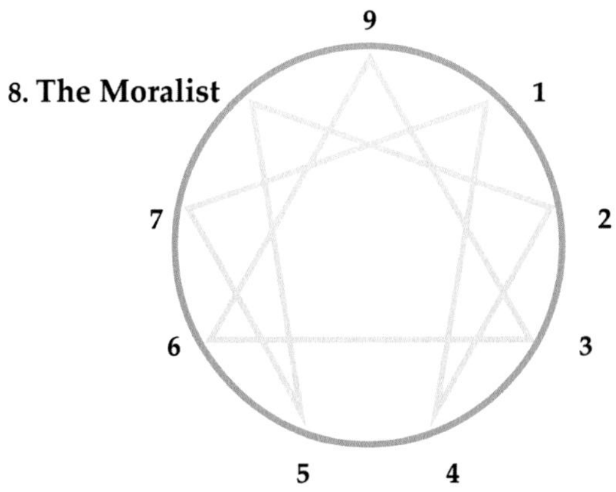

as an obscuration of the Form of Divine Truth, the main characteristic of the Moralist is to look for the Truth in the moral sense in their life and the lives of others, their own society, and the world at large. Because the Moralist is constantly evaluating everything from their moralizing point of view, they become merciless critics of others, but even more devastating and unforgiving critics of themselves. The Moralist will fall from time to time into bouts of self–criticism in such a way that by imagining themselves as being bad and doing wrong, a sense of uncontrolled sexual lasciviousness opens, followed by unending moral chastisement. The lack of Divine Truth makes the Moralist adopt an ego–position of being the final authority on moral, religious and political matters. They like to sermonize because deep inside themselves they feel very acutely the lack of Divine Truth and spiritual and moral authenticity. In general, they also lust to discipline others and are inclined to impose on others cruel moral sanctions, heartless judgment, and righteous indignation.

EGO–REDUCTION OF THE MORALIST

The triad of the Being Group formed by the Moralist (point

8), the Perfectionist (point 1), and the Seeker (point 9) has the general Existential Attitudes of Sadness and Depression. The Moralists, because of their projection about their mother, project themselves as having been morally abused, which provokes a form of corruption in them. The ego–delusion of the Moralist is that they are living in moral disarray because they are suffering the subjective manifestations of karmic effects that have a sort of vengeance, which they finally impose on themselves as well as on their proximate relatives and friends. The Passion of the Moralist is Lust, not only in its sexual manifestation, but in the sense of excess and exaggeration in everything they are doing as well. The Moralist lives in the Dichotomy of Self–denial on one side and Self–indulgence on the other, and thus they go from the extremes of asceticism and self–criticism to indulging themselves to excess. Rationalization is the self–serving and superficial Primary Defense Mechanism of the Moralist's over–critical stand to morally justify their excesses. This contrasts with their criticisms of the moral behavior of others. Moralists distort the facts, rationalizing their intolerant Feelings or actions by elaborating plausible motives or excuses to make these appear acceptable. Their ego–position is that of Self–criticism; they appear to be constantly self–righteous. The ego–balancer of the Moralist is in asserting to themselves "I am ethical and open–minded." The difficulty in their life is that they are constantly inhibited as a result of their self–criticism. Their ego–reaction to the situations of life and more particularly to the criticism of others is violence by word or deed. Their ego–justification is duplicity or astute explanations. The Moralist's Door of Compensation is Cruelty in their criticism of others and themselves. They constantly have the

Dichotomic Existential Attitudes of being Fair on one side and Critical on the other. Their way out is their search for true Redemption from their many real or supposed sins against themselves or others, and it is by this Way of Redemption that the Moralist falls into their own Trap, which is that of true Morality. Across this truly ethical state of morality, they will discover Divine Truth and enter into the State of contemplating the True, One, Eternal God.

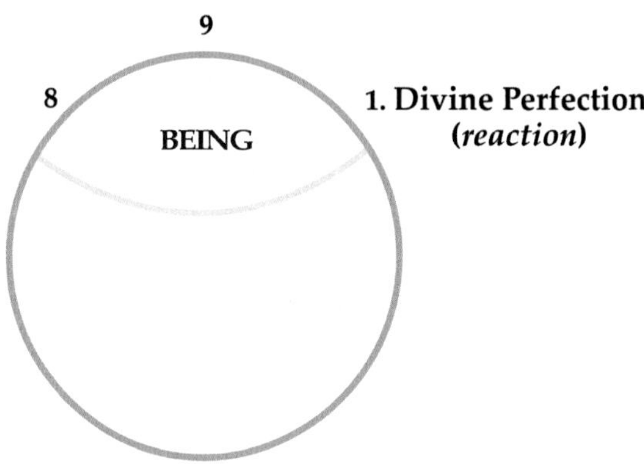

DIVINE PERFECTION (Point 1)

In the triad of the Being Group, Divine Perfection is the *reaction* (returning) point. This is to say, as Divine Truth (point 8) is the *action* (proceeding) point and imposes itself, so to speak, in the sheer manifestation of the Light of Innate Awareness and Consciousness, Divine Perfection, being the *reaction* (returning) point, collects the Objective Reality of Divine Truth and manifests it as Divine Perfection or a completeness of the process of being, and because it is perfect and complete, it will naturally return to the *result* (sustaining point) of the triad, Divine Love (point 9), which, at the same time, is the *result* and origin.

The Form of Divine Perfection, because it is the culmination of the Form of Divine Truth from which it actually proceeds, has a powerfully grounded and affirming quality that becomes the test of the Form of Divine Truth and also its measure in the sense of implying Totality in absolute terms. Because the Form of Divine Perfection points to the basic principle of aesthetic contemplation (an appreciation from the point of view of perfection), the ability to contemplate aesthetically depends on Divine Perfection as producing the perfect model in the sense of Divine Forms. This sense of discovering perfection everywhere is the most important attribute of The Beautiful, and it is this perfect State of The Beautiful that will develop into the Form of Divine Love, with the Form of Divine Perfection producing the contemplation of this Idea in the most ancient way of observing the perfection of the Universe on a starry night. While entering into one–pointed concentration with a chosen star, it is possible to open the State of Innate Awareness of the intrinsic and magnificent Divine Perfection of the entire Cosmos. When this happens, we enter into an Innate Awareness that the infinite Cosmos is just one Unity because it proceeds in harmonious Unity with a connection that reveals that the infinite Universe is a totally alive being, eternally open, and eternally present. Thus, by entering the Form of Divine Perfection, we open in ourselves the transcendental contemplation of the Infinite, Perfect Cosmos which is totally alive, permeated by the Spirit of God in the Form of the fundamental and primordial Consciousness that with Divine Perfection sustains the entire Universe with which it is one and the same and inseparable and, therefore, is Absolute Perfection. From the realization of the harmonious Unity of Cosmic perfection, humankind naturally reverts its point of view to itself and finds, by a simple process of discrimination, the realization that we, as human beings, are the only species able to become Self–realized, and thus, because we can contemplate ourselves as part of the Perfect Creation, it is logical to infer that in each one of us there is a synthesis of the entire process of the Universe from the very beginning, if any, until now.

Therefore, in human beings are reflected all the Laws of Cosmic evolution, and because we are beings that have completed our journey through nature and can become conscious of our own process, we can conceptualize ourselves as a microcosm, the alive and conscious synthesis of the macrocosm that is of Divine Perfection and Beauty; and by inference, human beings must have a divinely perfect Form of Divine Man. This is to say, we are a Divine Prototype that is totally perfect since the beginning of time, as a perfect model that exists naturally in all of us, and whose Divine Perfection is for us to attain by a process of letting go of our imperfect human personality or lower ego founded upon the Trifix of the Existential Mind (Sphere 15), and by a Method of clarification of consciousness of all obscurations of the Relative Mind to then enter into the Divine Perfection of the Divine Human Prototype. The recognition of this Perfection innate in all of us is a fundamental Divine Form toward the process of salvation, spiritual transcendence, and Knowledge of the perfect Truth, which is Gnosis or Transcendental Consciousness, an Innate Awareness that the Perfected permeates, as well as is The One and the All. This concept of perfection in human beings is in the sense of our Higher Self not only as a human perfection but a Divine Perfection because it is wholly spiritual, transcendent and thus, immaterial and of Divine Substance.

This is to say that Divine Perfection, as the second aspect (*reaction*) of the triad of the Being Group, like Divine Truth discovers, discloses and reveals the true ever–existing Being. This is a recognition of the most important characteristic or attribute of the Form of 'Being as such,' the primordial ontology or the disclosing of Being in the sense of Parmenides, who describes the 'Being as such' as a perfect conscious awareness of itself. This Innate Awareness of Perfect Being can be actualized only if we contemplate the total perfection of the 'Being as such.' As Parmenides observed in his famous poem *On Nature*, "the being is and can never not be." This is the First Principle of Formal Logic, whose formula is A=A. This is a tautological proposition: a subject that is explained by itself—a rose is a rose. Kant would establish that the truth of a tautology is such because it is an analytic proposition, it just analyzes itself. In this sense, analytical propositions, contrary to synthetic propositions, do not add any new knowledge about the subject (a rose is a rose).

But in the famous proposition of Parmenides, the Being is Being, which is an analytical proposition that has no other form of description because the Being—since it is Simple, One, Unchangeable, Transcendental, and Eternal—cannot be described by any other thing but itself. And the second proposition of Parmenides, that the Being cannot be not–Being, seals the proposition of identity with the Second Principle of Formal Logic, the Principle of Contradiction, which denies that the truth could be contradictory in any way. Further on, because the 'Being as such' can never enter into the 'process of becoming,' the possibility of the Being becoming not–Being is radicalized by the Third Principle of Formal logic, the Principle of the Excluded Middle. Thus, Being has to be itself without the possibility of ever appearing to contradict this identity. This in ontological terms is the Total Perfection of Being; in metaphysical terms, it is the Ultimate Reality; and in theological terms, it is the One Transcendental God.

Thus, the Form of Divine Perfection, as the principle that symphonizes the entire Cosmos, is basic for the idea of the microcosm that has to be 'perfect in itself,' because the microcosm, as the son of the Absolute Being, reflects the perfection of the father. This is the idea of the Divine Spark of the Orphics; the idea of the perfect number of the Pythagoreans; the number nine as the sum and perfection of the entire series of primary numbers; and in the Integral Theory the Pleroma of the nine Divine Forms manifesting the Transcendental Mind of the Divine Human Prototype. Therefore, the Form of Divine Perfection is fundamental for the Unity of a process in accordance with the Laws of Trialectics that demand that every process proceed upon perfect pre–established Laws and patterns. Here the Principle of Identity of Being of Formal Logic becomes in Trialectics the Law of Mutation: that every process develops in accordance with a pre–established pattern. Thus, Trialectics establishes, not the identity of the 'Being as such,' but the identity of the 'process of becoming,' and with the unifying second Law of Trialectics, the Law of Circulation, the Being and the becoming move from Being into not–Being and return to Being again, therefore superseding the Principle of Contradiction of Formal Logic.

Protoanalysis is defined as the analysis of the entire psyche considered in all its relative aspects across the Realms of Existence and Knowledge and the Domains of Consciousness and, by the practices of Integral Philosophy, we are able to be in relationship with the perfection of the Divine Human Prototype that is innate in all of us. Thus, with the clarification processes of Protoanalysis and the Integral Path of Philosophy, we can reestablish in ourselves the perfect and liberated Divine Human Prototype that is studied and experienced as the Divine Metatelos, the final goal of the Pure Spirit, totally and divinely awakened under the rule of the Form of Divine Perfection.

MENTATIONAL ANALYSIS OF DIVINE PERFECTION

1 **SUBSTANCE** (What is it?) Divine Perfection is the Innate Awareness and insight that Reality is innately perfect and that Reality is just what is. In the terms of Parmenides, the Being is and can never contradict itself by not–Being. This is to say, it is perfect. 'Reality in itself' has this condition of Being, and consequently is perfect. Thus, Divine Perfection appears in everything, moment to moment, if the process is observed from the point of view of the whole or the Unity of the Totality.

2 **FORM** (How is it?) The Idea of Divine Perfection manifests as the 'Being as such' which is perfect, real and complete.

3 **POSSIBILITIES** (Why originated?) The Unity of God is the Ultimate Perfection.

4 **NEEDS** (What purpose?) Divine Perfection is the foundation of the 'State of Mind–only' by the Innate Awareness that 'reality as such' is perfect.

5 **IMPULSE** (What intention?) Divine Perfection reflects the Unity of Reality in the State of Pure Consciousness or 'Mind–only.'

6 **METHOD** (How accomplished?) Divine Perfection is the contemplation and insight into a Mind without the obscurations of duality and thinking.

7 **STANDARD** (What is the ideal?) Divine Perfection is the 'Being as such.'

8 **ORIENTATION** (What is the direction?) Divine Perfection is oriented toward the absolute completeness of Divine Love.

9 **CAPACITY** (What is the strength?) The strength of Divine Perfection arises from the fact that everything in reality is perfect and thus, presents the universality of this Divine Form that can be found everywhere.

10 **CHARISMA** (What is the appearance?) When entering into the State of clear Innate Awareness, we find the Divine Perfection of the Pure Light of Consciousness.

11 **MEANS** (How produced?) Divine Perfection can only be approached with the clear Innate Awareness of Consciousness that can reflect Reality as it is in its intrinsic Perfection.

12 **GOALS** (What is attained?) The attainment of Divine Perfection is the deepest insight into the Unity of all.

THE FIXATION OF THE PERFECTIONIST

The Form of Divine Perfection in the correlative Enneagram of the Fixations in the Existential Mind (Sphere 15) has the

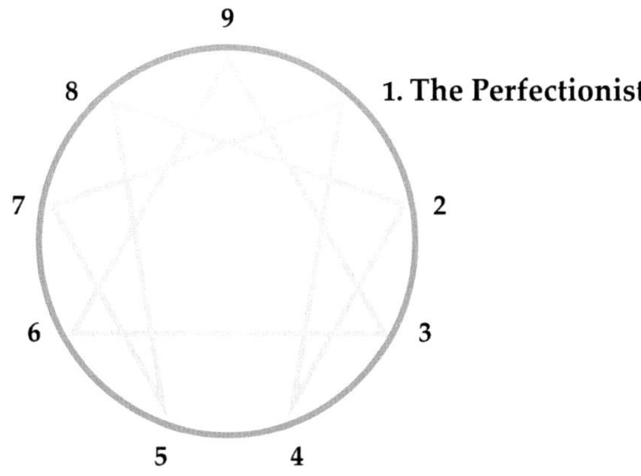

Ego–Fixation of the Perfectionist. This Ego–Fixation developed in childhood by the influence of a mother who appeared to the child as a distant, rigid, cold, and unloving person, and who seemed to constantly observe all the defects—real and apparent—in the child and the child's behavior. Thus, because of the deep feeling of actually lacking perfection, the child develops the fixated idea of not being perfect enough and then develops a profound self–righteousness based on preconceived patterns of perfection that only make their Ego–Fixation more acute. It can be recognized by their characteristic punctiliousness, meticulousness and fastidious behavior. The Perfectionist has to be understood as being obsessed with obtaining perfection in every area of their life, as well as in their personal behavior and being. Because they belong to the Being Group, they are influenced by the general Existential Attitudes of Sadness, Depression and a "broken heart," and this will make them resentful about the lack of perfection in others, but even more acutely this lack of perfection in themselves.

EGO–REDUCTION OF THE PERFECTIONIST

Because the Perfectionist is an Ego–Fixation that has its source in the projection of an unloving mother who is distant and demands perfection, Perfectionists feel themselves as being unloved, which provokes Depression. Their main ego–delusion is based on the attitude of Resentment against the world and themselves. This constant Resentment generates in them the Passion of Anger; they will thrill themselves by producing in their imagination angry scenes and violent confrontations. Their Dichotomy is to be Callous on one side and Touchy on the other. Their Primary Defense Mechanism is Isolation. When a feeling or situation is unacceptable, Perfectionists defend or distance themselves from psychic distress by isolating themselves from it. They isolate themselves by being cold and unloving, especially to those who have provoked their anger, and also because they feel that they are not loved. Their ego–position is that of Self–righteousness. The ego–balancer of the Perfectionist is "I am responsive and adaptive." Their difficulty is their sense of being resented by others and themselves. The ego–reaction of the Perfectionist is that of weakness, regardless of their imagined reckless confrontations. Their ego–justification is a stubbornness that affirms their own ego–position. The Perfectionist uses the Door of Compensation of Toximania as a means to palliate their extreme sense of imperfection and depression in finding themselves unlovable and isolated. Their Dichotomic Existential Attitudes are Objective on one side and Judgmental on the other. Their way out is Attention, because the Perfectionist's natural inclination is to pay attention to the details of whatever they see, experience or achieve, and it is by way of this Attention that they discover and realize that perfection is everywhere in the very moment that they stop projecting their sense of imperfection.

The Perfectionist will find their own Trap, the desire for Perfection, which will open the Form of Divine Perfection that can dissolve their Fixation.

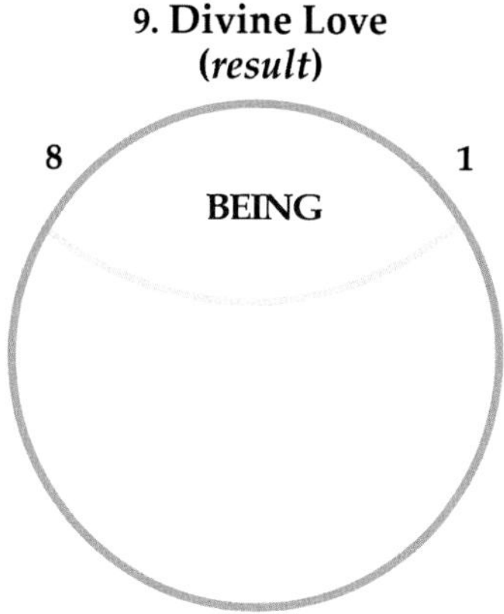

DIVINE LOVE (Point 9)

Divine Love is the resulting (sustaining) point, where the function of the triad of the Being Group is supported. In this case, it is the Super Form or Idea of Being. So Divine Love can be defined as where the fullness of Being abides. This implies that it appears as a consequence or the result of the Innate Awareness of the Truth of Divine Existence (point 8), which is then absorbed by the reaction (returning) point as Divine Perfection (point 1) that contemplates and finds that the entire Creation is The Good.

This Innate Goodness of Reality, when appreciated fully, appears as Divine Love, the *resulting* (sustaining) point (point 9). Thus, Divine Love actually means finding, from the point of view of God, that everything in His Creation is The Good. When the Form of Divine Love opens, it can appear only in a

Non–conceptual Mind that is looking at Reality as it is, and by finding it true, perfect and good, this State of Mind has a love for the entire Creation. Therefore love, as a product of the contemplation of the Form of Divine Love, appears as an Innate Awareness of a profound clarity in the Mind and an infinitely blissful feeling in the heart, nourishing it, and becoming a sense of happiness in the solar plexus and well–being in the Kath or *tan t'ien* (Chn), the point of energy or *chi* generation in the body, three finger–widths below the navel.

It has to be noted that this love is not the product of the subjectivity of the Trifix which has preferences and aversions, as well as the discriminative duality of judging reality as being good or bad. Divine Love, as a Divine Form, is Transcendental and Universal. Thus, it can only relate with what is objectively existing as Reality as it is. Only this perfectly impartial Mind will naturally abide by entering into the Form of Divine Love. Because Divine Love is point 9 of the enneagram, it is the Divine Form that contains the other eight. Thus, it can be said that the whole Enneagram of Divine Forms (Ideas) encompasses all facets or aspects of Divine Love.

When Divine Love is attained, it is found to be inexhaustible; this only increases with practice, producing a brilliance and a happiness in life for the simple truth that, by finding everything good and lovable, we permeate ourselves with the life–giving power of Divine Love. This transcendental experience that provokes the contemplation of Divine Love is the most direct path to the Innate Awareness of the Divine Love of God, which gives us real Being with its total Divine Truth and Divine Perfection.

The Form of Divine Love is sustained by the Super Form of God, the Supreme Good before whom there can be nothing better. This Supreme Good is the love of God toward His Good Creation with humanity as part of it. This Supreme Good becomes the desire of all creation to unite with it, and because it is Divine Good, love arises from the heart of all humans in an unstoppable love and desire for The Good. This love for The Good is what makes us emulate the same Good of the Beloved, and this is the most powerful, transformative and transmutative power of Divine Love, the most immediate of the Divine Forms of the Pleroma or the Totality of the Godhead.

In Plato's *Symposium,* Socrates exposes the 'doctrine of Divine Love and the Supreme Divine Good or God' by way of the speech of the Priestess Diotima, who initiated Socrates into the understanding that we could attain the final degree of Union with the Supreme Good only and exclusively by way of "true love" of the Divine Good God. Thus, the last realization in the spiritual and mystical road to The Good has to necessarily be by desiring it with a devotion that can only be promoted and actualized by Divine Love, which is capable of finding God and The Good in everything and everybody in His Creation. This natural expansiveness of the Form of Divine Love permeates our entire Soul with the Divine Good of the One Absolute God.

This expanding Divine Love from the Good God that permeates the entire Universe in the mode of the Divine Providential Spirit transforms the human Soul completely to the point that this love starts expanding from the heart of human beings to everybody, every sentient being, and everything in the Universe. As Empedocles said in his famous poem, "God is Omnipresent, God is Love, all we need is love." Then Empedocles adds a negative and somehow hopeless line, "Unfortunately, man does not know or recognize what love is." The negative part here serves the definition of love as one that can be recognized only in a State of Self–awareness by which we can understand and see the world as it really is and thus, finding it truthful and real, perfect and beautiful, we becomprofoundly attracted with true love for everything, and therefore become actual generators of the love of the Divine toward everybody and everything.

This Form of Divine Love in the Platonic sense lost its importance and was replaced by the scientifically oriented Epicureans and Atomists, but it was rediscovered by the Stoics as the *Logos* (Gk), the Word or the Logos of God, which is essentially the actual Creator of the Universe by way of His Divine Love. This is the Divine Love that we have to reawaken in the human heart. It was only much later in the sixteenth century, at the beginning of the Italian Renaissance, that the Florentine Platonists Marsilio Ficino and Pico della Mirandola developed the theory that the love of The Beautiful and the love of real art promote a sense of unattached love, which is pure admiration that is conducive to the understanding of Pure Love, and in that way, as in the discourse of Socrates' Priestess Diotima, this Objective Love will attach its Innate Awareness to Divine Love or the Supreme Good God.

MENTATIONAL ANALYSIS OF DIVINE LOVE

1 **SUBSTANCE** (What is it?) Love is the natural condition of the mind actualized by a Mind of Non–conceptualization that is beyond duality. Divine Love can be apprehended only by the Absolute Mind, itself apprehended by a Mind of Calm–abiding and Pure Light of Innate Awareness. The substance of Divine Love is its life–giving power to the entire Cosmos.

2 **FORM** (How is it?) Divine Love is the contemplation of the Goodness and the Divine Love of Ultimate Reality as it is. It has the form of profound bliss, happiness and well–being.

3 **POSSIBILITIES** (Why originated?) The origin of Divine Love can be found in the Innate Awareness of the Divine Truth of the existence of the Divine, and in the Perfected State from which Divine Love arises.

4 **NEEDS** (What purpose?) Since, as Empedocles said, "All you need is love," the purpose of Divine Love is none other than the plentifulness of life, bliss and happiness.

5 **IMPULSE** (What intention?) Divine Love fundamentally is life, Light and Knowledge.

6 **METHOD** (How accomplished?) Divine Love is accomplished by the contemplation of Divine Truth and Divine Perfection.

7 **STANDARD** (What is the ideal?) Divine Love sustains and is a manifestation of the Unity of all.

8 **ORIENTATION** (What is the direction?) Divine Love dissolves all opposition and contradiction because it is oriented to the Universal and the Absolute.

9 **CAPACITY** (What is the strength?) Divine Love, as point 9 of the Enneagram of Divine Forms, contains the other eight points.

10 **CHARISMA** (What is the appearance?} Divine Love appears as the *result* of Divine Truth, Divine Perfection, and the contemplation of The Beautiful.

11 **MEANS** (How produced?) Divine Love appears by the opening of the Mind to Divine Truth and Divine Perfection, which results in the opening of the heart to Divine Love.

12 **GOALS** (What is attained?) The attainment of Divine Love is the apprehension of the splendor of the Unity of the Good God.

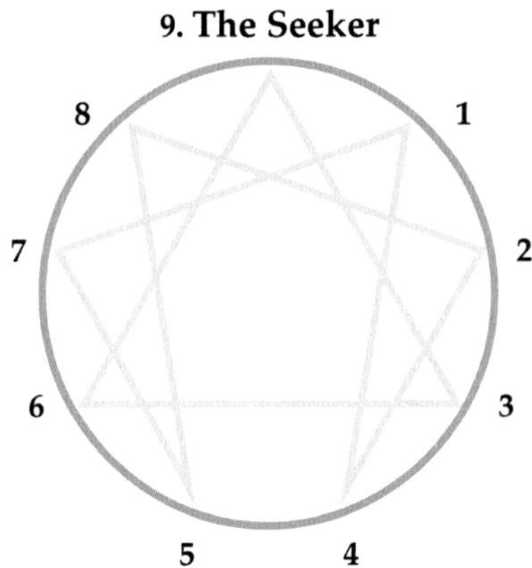

THE FIXATION OF THE SEEKER

This profound Objective Love is not connected to the attachment of subjective preferences which are just serving self–interest or to what, in fact, is the egocentric point of view of the fixated point 9, the Seeker, in the Enneagram of the Fixations of the Existential Mind (Sphere 15). The Seeker is the Ego–Fixation that in the triad of the Being Group is the *resulting* or sustaining point, and consequently the source and pinnacle of the triad formed by the Moralist (point 8), the Perfectionist (point 1), and the Seeker (point 9). In accordance with Protoanalysis, the fixated point of the Seeker appears as a manifestation of the subjective aspects of the Existential Attitudes of the Conservation Instinct: Sadness, Depression and a "broken heart." The Moralist feels abused, the Perfectionist feels unloved, and the Seeker feels abandoned as an outcome of the Existential Attitudes. The Seeker has to be understood in the Protoanalytical sense as rather an ironic description of the tragedy–comedy and clown–like characteristics of the Ego–Fixations in general. The loss of the Form of Divine Love produces a devastating effect of being unloved and unappreciated, making the Seeker feel that, in reality, this is because they are no good, not beautiful, or imperfect. They have no real self–value, making this Ego–Fixation live in a constant search for that remote love which is always just imagined or intuited, but never really discovered. What throws the Seeker into a new search is a profound attitude of discouragement with dark tones of a constant heartbroken reaction to the world.

Divine Love also means life, for there is no life without love. In accordance with Protoanalysis, our first impression of life is consequently our most basic and primordial perception of the world by way of our Spiritual Pole. Its Spiritual Drive is basically love and, if the child comes to find a rather unloving, rejecting, cruel, and deceitful world, love becomes canceled in its pure manifestation in the child. This, as we have seen, will affect the Conservation Instinct, which forms the triad of the

Being Group of the Ego–Fixations. This sense of rejection felt in the Spiritual Pole appears as a feeling of being abandoned, of actually being cut off in the most intimate sense of self–preservation. This will produce a lack of the sense of being and will become a constant feeling of self–depreciation and low self–esteem, because the child will perceive that they do not merit love or that they are not lovable, and consequently they must not be a good person, and because of that, they will feel rejected and abandoned. During adolescence and adult life, these feelings will appear as a profound and incurable sadness, a "broken heart," and a constant depression, and these feelings will develop into a neurosis that will use the Defense Mechanism of Compensation, blaming the entire world for their poor and sad internal state of affairs. But basically the feeling that the cruel world is against them is nothing but the lack of the Form of Divine Love, now replaced by the fixated point of the Seeker with their constant search for love, understanding and appreciation of their internal being, their sense of being something and of having some value genuinely and authentically because, with the Existential Attitudes of sadness and depression, these individuals appear as having a "broken heart." Divine Love is the absolute cure and the antidote for the fixated point of the Seeker (point 9). It is an openness to the world that cures the primordial Spiritual Drive which can now flow as Divine Love from the Mind and the heart in the State of Divine Love.

EGO–REDUCTION OF THE SEEKER

Because the Seeker projects that their mother abandoned them and they felt uncared for, which provokes suffering in them, they feel themselves sad, depressed and "broken–hearted" in the manifestations of their Existential Attitudes. Their ego–delusion is that of seeing the world with an attitude of Indolence or an indifference in their fundamental approach to life. The Passion of the Seeker is Laziness and sloth in the sense of a general lack of caring about the world and themselves. Their Dichotomy is Skeptical on one side and Gullible on the other. Seekers use the Primary Defense Mechanism of Compensation by which Feelings of subordination, frustration or failure in one field are compensated by achievement in another in order to reinforce their self-esteem and self-image. For example, they may compensate for inadequacies in their family relations by developing outside friendships. Their Feelings of deficiencies are compensated by seeking thrills and entertainment, and trying to feel compensated by friendships. Their ego–position is Self–pity with a constant string of complaints. The ego–balancer of the Seeker is "I am spiritual and realistic," which affirms some sense of True Reality. The Seeker's difficulty is their constant indecisiveness. Their ego–reaction is to be disillusioned about everything—personal relations and events. The ego–justification of the Seeker is Pity where they feel sorry for everyone's situation, including their own. The Seeker uses the Door of Compensation of Sensuality in order to relieve their depressed and sad existence. Their Dichotomic Existential Attitude on one side is Supportive and on the other Sarcastic. The way out for the Seeker is the constant analysis of themselves in order to find Self–awareness. The Trap of the Seeker is Seeking for love, which will open the Form of Divine Love that will dissolve their Fixation and its process.

CHAPTER 3

THE LIVING GROUP

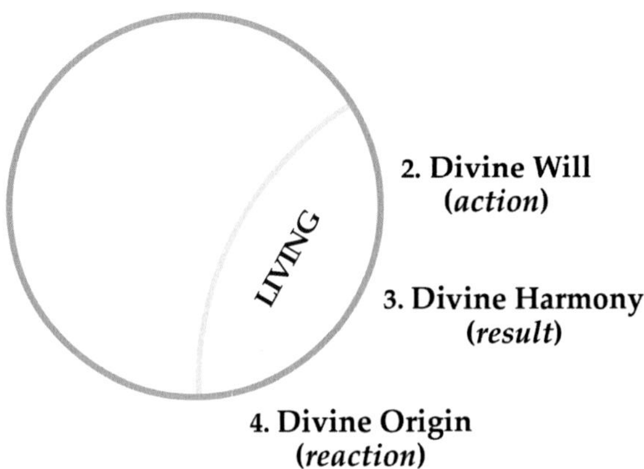

TRIAD OF THE LIVING GROUP

The triad of the Living Group is the manifestation of the Super Form of the Good Man. The Good Man produces the 'good life' and the 'good life' promotes a Good Society. It is upon the Good Man that it is possible to make a Good Life, and we find that this consists of a virtuous life, for only in virtue is it possible to find The Good. Thus, the triad of the Living Group, as a manifestation of the Super Form of the Good Man which is found in the virtuous life, is an ethical triad and, therefore, all three Divine Forms reflect profound ethical concepts that are to be found in the higher Illuminative Mind (Sphere 6), whose content is the Enneagram of the Integral Virtues.

The triad of the Living Group is composed of Divine Will (point 2), Divine Origin (point 4), and Divine Harmony (point 3). In the internal function of this triad, Divine Will (point 2) is the *action* point, Divine Origin (point 4) is the *reaction* point, and Divine Harmony (point 3) is the *resulting* point. The function of the triad is the Super Ethical Form of the Good Man. The triad of the Living Group has the three Divine Forms that are the basis of all ethical concepts. The Form of Divine Will, which is found only in Perfect Freedom, is the basic concept of the ethics of Kant and his 'doctrine of Practical Reason,' by which real will is found only in Perfect Freedom. It is only in this freedom where the 'will of God' can appear as a categorical imperative or a complete demand to be followed by the acceptance of a free consciousness. Thus, the Kantian concept of duty has to be taken and accepted freely. Therefore, Divine Will is the manifestation and the *action* (proceeding) of the Divine Form of the ethical force of the Good Man. Next, Divine Origin (point 4) is the *reaction* point that goes back to the authentic source of the ethical Good Man. Divine Harmony (point 3) is the *resulting* (sustaining) point of the triad, and it harmonizes Divine Will and the freedom of its manifestation with Divine Origin, the Source of all, which dictates its own Absolute Will as Creator. This becomes harmonized by the Form of Divine Harmony or Divine Law which produces the unity between the freedom of man and the necessity of Divine Providence.

As in the triad of the Divine Forms of the Living Group, in which the *function* is the Super Form of the Good Man, in the correlative Enneagram of the Fixations, the *function* is the Relation Instinct which deals with the interrelation and communication of a human society. As an Instinct, it is fundamental for our survival, since we obviously cannot survive without our society. The Instincts are directly influenced and conditioned by the Polar Preconception of finding a rejecting, wicked and deceitful world, which is then answered by the warlike and aggressive preconception of the Spiritual and Sexual Poles acting through the manifestation of force and vitality to conquer or attract this wicked world. The Polar Preconception manifests in the Relation Instinct as the Existential Attitude of being Angry and Anxious with the world. A person with this Existential Attitude appears to have a "chip on their shoulder," and they are ready to be disappointed and to react angrily, while living constantly in a state of anxiety provoked by projections toward other human beings. This Existential Attitude of the Living Group will trigger the manifestations of the fixated points with the consequent loss of the Divine Forms.

Integral Philosophy establishes that when a Divine Form is lost, all the Divine Forms are lost at the same time. Consequently, when a fixated point becomes established, the entire set of the Ego–Fixations becomes present and active, replacing the Divine Forms. More specifically, this movement happens three times, once in each triad, thereby forming the new triadic system of the Ego–Fixations or the Trifix. The anger and anxiety that are so clear during childhood and adolescence become in adult life a neurotic system that has, as a Defense Mechanism, Aggression by word or deed, and a constant attitude that "I know better." In this way the Existential Attitude blocks the Divine Form and produces the obscuration of the Form of Divine Will, which is the actual observance of Reality with its homogeneous Laws and forces, and instead the Divine Form is replaced by an attitude of independence, defiance and mistrust, in the form of the Ego–Fixation of the Independent (point 2). The Form of Divine Origin is replaced by the fixated

Reasoner (point 4) who, instead of looking directly to the Divine Origin of all, rationalizes everything, finds superfluous causes, and in this way loses the view of the big picture; and finally, by the Existential Attitudes of Anger and Anxiety, the Form of Divine Harmony with its profound sense of justice and equality is lost. It is replaced by the Ego–Fixation of the Displayer (point 3) who, instead of looking for the harmony of the Laws, presents themself as the model and the law with their superior pretentiousness of facing the world, with the accompanying attitude of having a "chip on the shoulder" and a readiness against the constant wrongdoings of all humankind and society.

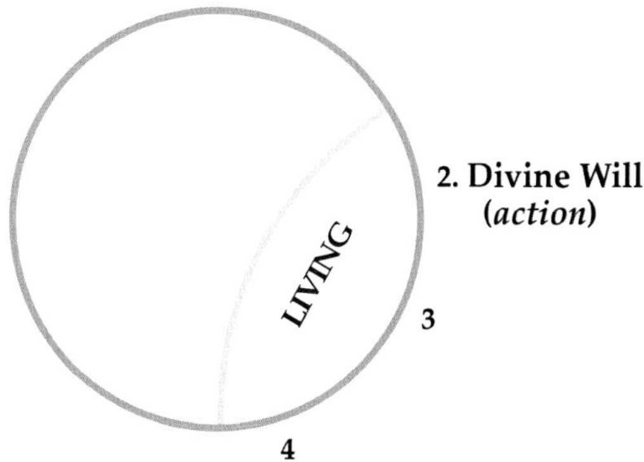

DIVINE WILL (Point 2)

The Form of Divine Will appears in its Pure State in the Primordial Mind (Sphere 16) as the efficient cause of the pure Spiritual Drive of the Spiritual Pole, whose purpose is to obtain knowledge and harmonious Universal understanding. The Form of Divine Will can be understood only in correlation with the theistic Form of Divine Providence, which is characterized as the innate natural force of the Goodness of God toward His Creation which can sustain the 'process of becoming' and is unchanged in accordance with the internal desire of being, existing and knowing. This 'will to be' is the superior manifestation of the force of survival. The other manifestation is the Sexual Drive of the Sexual Pole, whose purpose is the survival of life through the renewal of generations. Thus, the 'will to be,' which is the innate cause of the Spiritual Drive of the Spiritual Pole, is the most primordial manifestation of Divine Providence in the sense of giving the strength of the 'will to be,' or the 'will to live,' or the 'will to power.' This innermost will is the will to discover what it is that does not change and is complete, thus becoming the ultimate goal of survival—the 'Being as such' by which we enter into the Eternity of the Spirit and consequently into immortality.

Divine Will, as Divine Providence, manifests throughout the Cosmos as the Laws of Reality, which are pre-established. To attune with this Divine Will was the ultimate goal of the Ethical schools of the Ancients, especially Panaetius, a Middle Stoic of the second century BC, and his great disciple Posidonius, who unified the 'will of God' with the Astral religion of the Chaldeans and the Zoroastrian Magi. For Posidonius, the influence of the stars and the knowledge of their perfect cycles was the actual scripture of Divine Providence or Divine Will. Thus, Divine Will (*action*) depends on and is sustained by the Form of Divine Harmony (*result*) and it has the *reaction* (returning) point of Divine Origin, the Source of all. Therefore, the Form of Divine Will can be found only in the freedom and harmony of all. In that point, we find the force of The Good of the Creation permeating everything, but to enter into Divine Will we must first attain a condition of Total Freedom.

As Aristotle says in his *Nicomachean Ethics,* moral judgment, ethical conduct, and virtue can exist only in the condition of Total Freedom of the subject. Any influence that limits the freedom of the subject by whatever means—physical, emotional, mental, or spiritual—corrupts and taints the pure act of freedom of choice in accordance with ethical principles. This supreme importance of freedom, specifically pointed out by Aristotle, was later developed by the Stoics Zeno of Citium, Cleanthes and Chrysippus, with the doctrine that the freedom of man supremely consists of the Total Freedom of Mind. This is a mind free from material attachments, the lower emotions, and judgmental and envious thoughts. This purified Mind could attain the Transcendental Ground where all the Virtues are supported. This principle states that only a mind beyond good and evil, without the influence of prejudices and social mores, can attain the Divine Virtues of the gods and can become by this influence a Soul that can reflect real spirituality. The Stoics knew this perfected man as the Wise Man or the Sage who, because of his perfection of living in a Divine State, could not be polluted by any sort of mistake or corruption that could obscure the Soul. He was beyond good and evil.

The idea that freedom is possible only in a state of relation with God's Providence or His Will was asserted by Spinoza in his *Ethics*. This was reaffirmed by Kant who, like Aristotle, makes freedom the condition for producing a State of Mind that can understand the absolute spiritual morality of the categoric imperative, the moral principle which has the ethical force of imposing itself as a command in the sense of categorical and as a duty in the sense of imperative or unavoidable. Thus, Kant finds in freedom the transcendentality of the Spirit where, by being free from all personal interests, it could raise man to the level where he could produce an ethical command that has the characteristic of being Universal, therefore becoming an unavoidable duty whose choice has been produced by a liberated consciousness. Or, if we go back to the Stoic proposition from which Kant was inspired, one might attain the freedom of the Sage who, because he was above material interests and emotional attachments, could follow the Universal Will of Divine Providence in the form of Laws and principles that could be discovered in reality; the Sage, by not opposing them, would absorb the will of what is Divine and spiritual. He could always follow the Universal Will or the Divine Providence and, therefore, he could not fall into error or mistakes, because all his acts depended entirely on the 'will of God.'

Nietzsche, as modern scholars observe, also followed the Stoic model of the Sage when producing his *Zarathustra* and his more mature work *Beyond Good and Evil*, where the principles of social morality are founded upon religious principles, which moralize and judge about what is good or evil, and which have to be deconstructed into their origin where we can find the interests that are serving the prejudicial religious stand and, with this deconstruction of morality, we can attain a state of pure self–responsibility, free from prejudices and preconceptions. This is a mind able in its freedom to follow its innate 'will to power' or will toward that energy that is universally oriented to produce life instead of death and thus, able to follow the most basic and Universal command of survival. Therefore, this fundamental Stoic proposition of finding the Superior Self, in which alone exist the Universal Principles, has profoundly affected the modern conception of the Mind of Pure Immediate Present, which opens for us a spaciousness of mind or the sense of infinity which is not temporal because it is Eternal.

This is what Husserl treats with his Phenomenological method, the reduction of all phenomena into a mind beyond phenomena, which he calls the "eidetic world," the world of *eideia* (Gk) or the Eternal Essences or Forms in the Platonic sense. Heidegger would say that the phenomenological reduction of Husserl should be applied to time and human temporality, with its three moments of past, present and future. These moments, when reduced into the mind beyond phenomena, will leave the present moment as real existential freedom, a freedom that means authenticity of consciousness, with consciousness being reduced to its simplicity and consequently its Pure Being, whose transcendentality is discovered by disclosing that behind the horizon of phenomena and in the perfect present, it is free from phenomenological obstructions and becomes the existential freedom of the Spirit.

Jean–Paul Sartre follows a parallel or two–sided analysis where real freedom is acquired: first, there is the relationship of 'being–for–other' (acting, being or doing for another person or in a state of dependence and slavery); and second, the relationship in the position of a consciousness that finds its being, a 'being for itself' thus, a being that is in a situation of non–dependency and therefore of complete freedom. This freedom becomes authentic only if it means living in the present time in a mind that has abstracted the process of time that demands the process of thinking, since thinking can manifest only in time. What Sartre is telling us in this very complicated figure is what he means by present being, which is nothing other than a mind of non–conceptualization and thus, it is beyond reasoning. Because this mind of pure present is not thinking or conceptualizing, it is not making objects of reality, including people, which unconsciously we make into things or into objects of our own making. This is a process of endless subjective presuppositions that make us dependent on our mental constructions, thoughts or dreams. To free ourselves from this existential dependency, because we are actually existing as depending and 'being–for–other,' we can only experience that freedom in the present 'here and now' without depending on the objectivized world of phenomena.

When we recognize ourselves in this fashion, we find ourselves thrown from nowhere into this actual existence, and suddenly the entire reality that is nothing but our own preconceptions loses total value and sense and, because of that, all that is left to us is a void that is a nothingness in the sense of having no purpose or justification for our existence. This obscurity of life that does not give us any guidance or direction is, in reality, a nothingness when we discover that these thoughts are our own preconceptions, and we are thrown into complete and total freedom, wanted or not. Thus, we have no alternative but to take our freedom, which makes us authentic, real and consequently responsible. Therefore, Sartre equates freedom with existential responsibility, and this freedom belongs uniquely to us. This leaves us facing the reality that our freedom has to take command and total responsibility for our destiny. For Sartre, there is not the consolation, as was the case for Pascal, of a Transcendental Divinity, which makes sense of the material absurdity that our own freedom has discovered about the world. Thus, our existence is our freedom and our own play over nothing. For us, we ourselves can make authentic sense of the world only if we can take the responsibility. This, at first, produces a vertigo, a fear, and a nausea at finding that we are so deprived and alone.

Therefore, in Integralism, the Form of Divine Will and Divine Freedom are the two aspects of the Super Form of Divine Good manifested as Divine Will in the Form of Divine Grace, capable of freeing the Soul from all obscurations, hindrances and fetters. These obscurations disturb Divine Will in the sense of our knowing the Providence of God directing us to the Supreme Freedom of the Mind that encounters itself as its only and unique object, thus producing a freedom of clarity and also a freedom that can be existentially real only in a State of Transcendental Freedom of the Mind. Divine Will is the level of a liberated Mind, free from the obscurations of karma that provoke suffering, which is the basic condition of a mind that is imprisoned in the gigantic labyrinth of its own subjective and Relative Mind.

MENTATIONAL ANALYSIS OF DIVINE WILL

1 **SUBSTANCE** (What is it?) Divine Will means the ability to emanate The Good from the point of view of Total Freedom, which means perfect detachment from karma and subjectivity.

2 **FORM** (How is it?) When free of karma and subjectivity, we can contemplate the Form of Divine Will as Divine Providence.

3 **POSSIBILITIES** (Why originated?) Divine Will has its origin in the Absolute Good.

4 **NEEDS** (What purpose?) The innate purpose of Divine Will is to reach the fullness of The Good.

5 **IMPULSE** (What intention?) Divine Will has the inner impulse of serving Divine Origin and Divine Harmony.

6 **METHOD** (How accomplished?) The understanding of Divine Will emerges with the freedom from karmic obscurations.

7 **STANDARD** (What is the ideal?) Divine Will has as its own standard the Unity of The Good.

8 **ORIENTATION** (What is the direction?) Divine Will is oriented toward the returning of the Spirit to its own Source of Light.

9 **CAPACITY** (What is the strength?) Divine Will has the strength of producing coherence and continuity in the process of life.

10 **CHARISMA** (What is the appearance?) When Divine Will is present, we are free from the subjectivity of our crude sense of being independent and separate. Divine

Will restores what is natural and does not intrude or interfere with the process.

11 **MEANS** (How produced?) Divine Will is the force toward the ultimate human purpose of entering into Divine Freedom.

12 **GOALS** (What is attained?) With Divine Will, there is attained the 'will to be' and the realization of the Spirit and immortality by the 'will to freedom' and complete Self–realization.

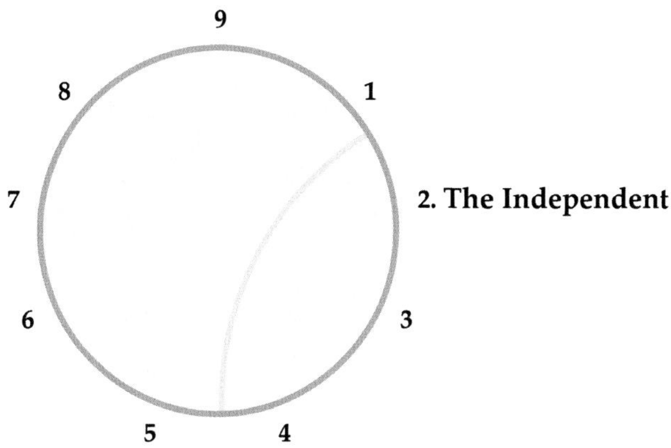

THE FIXATION OF THE INDEPENDENT

Correlative to the Enneagram of the Divine Forms, which are the content of the Creative Mind (Sphere 7), there is the Enneagram of the Fixations that corresponds to the Existential Mind (Sphere 15). Thus, the Form of Divine Will (point 2) in the Enneagram of Divine Forms has its correlative fixated point 2 of the Independent in the Enneagram of the Fixations. When in this ego–position, Divine Will has been replaced by the fixated point 2, the Independent, which, instead of freely contemplating reality as it is, tries to impose their own point of view of being independent, in the sense of being unreachable and consequently untouchable. As with every other Ego–Fixation, this means an actual imprisonment of a mind that is dominated by the influence of the Existential Attitudes; here, the Living Group triad of anger and anxiety shows the attitude of having a "chip on the shoulder" and "I am independent and could care less about anybody." When this sense of distorted independence is opened by the Form of Divine Will, a State of Liberation or a State of Divine Freedom is attained which is capable of recognizing and embodying Divine Will by following the flow and rules of the process.

EGO–REDUCTION OF THE INDEPENDENT

Because of projected emotions of being controlled by their father which provokes ignorance in them, the Independent has the Existential Attitudes of Anger, Anxiety and a "chip on the shoulder," with which they question anyone who wants to control them by imposing their own values. Their ego–delusion is that of acting as a self–appointed individual who, from a point of arrogance, manages relationships using Flattery with a profound sense of patronizing. The Passion of the Independent is Pride; they consider themselves unique and special. Their Dichotomy is Fussy on one side and Messy on the other. The Primary Defense Mechanism of the Independent is Denial in which they unconsciously refuse to recognize their projections of a father who they think overpowers, humiliates, controls, and reduces them. When confronted by any direction, Independents refuse to take responsibility for their own shortcomings or admit to their mistakes. Denial of illness or addiction is a common defense mechanism. Their ego–position is being Self–centered. The Independent affirms their life by the ego–balancer of "I am accommodating and organized." Their difficulty is the tendency to be frustrated by the performance of others. The ego–reaction of the Independent is to be dependent upon themselves and no one else. Their ego–justification is that of insolence and arrogance in order to maintain self–control. The Door of Compensation in order to balance the frustrations of the Independent is Psychosomatic Illness, from migraine headaches, ulcers and spastic colon to asthma and angina. Their Dichotomic Existential Attitudes are to be Encouraging on one side and Demanding on the other. The Independent will find their way out by understanding that their real Liberty is inherent to the human condition, and this will cause the Fixation to fall into its own Trap, the search for Freedom. This search for Freedom will open the Form of Divine Will, which will eliminate the Fixation of the Independent.

DIVINE ORIGIN (Point 4)

The Form of Divine Origin is the *reaction* (returning) point of the triad of the Living Group. Because it is an expression or an aspect of the Super Form of the Good Man, Divine Origin becomes the guide and provides the Higher Perspective to a process that, as such, has its beginning in the Source and a process that ends in the Source. With this State of Innate Awareness of the Form of Divine Origin, the Idea of Transcendentality appears clearly on the horizon, and the entire spiritual journey becomes enlightened by directing the entire process toward the origin or, more precisely, toward the natural State of Mind, which has the original clarity and fullness of the Absolute Mind, presenting itself as the origin and Source of the Relative

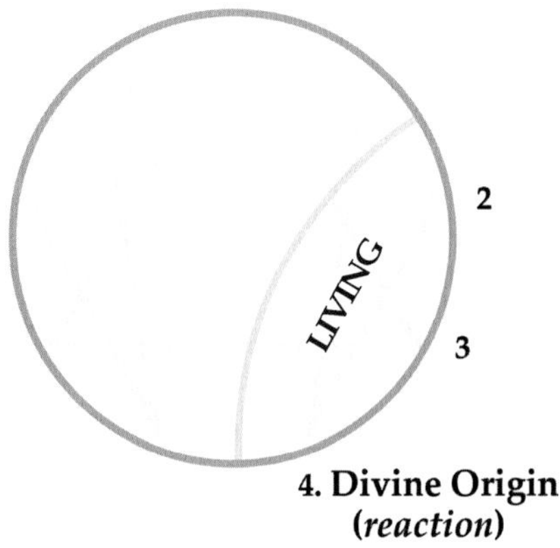

4. Divine Origin
(*reaction*)

Mind. Because of this, the Source, as both origin of the process and as the goal of the process, becomes united, because we find that the Source, the Absolute Mind, and the process of appearances of the Relative Mind are one and the same. This insight into the Unity and Transcendence of being and the 'process of becoming'—in which, at the end, being is totalized again—shows that we can always return to the contemplation of Absolute Being through the contemplation that the Relative 'becoming of appearances' or thought constructions are only manifestations of the Source or the 'Being as such.' Thus, in a profound way, the insight that gives us Divine Origin is the antidote and cure for the fixated Reasoner (point 4) who, because of the lack of the guide of Divine Origin or Source, becomes completely disoriented, making the most important task of its entire psyche that of obtaining reasons about the causes of things, in a constant "why?" that opens the Reasoner to new questions indefinitely. This lack of the Form of Divine Origin makes the Reasoner feel and look extremely disoriented, emotional and anxious to find their way in their living in society and their interconnection with other human beings, whom they paradoxically will find and describe as particularly disoriented without the knowledge of the real cause of the situations and events in their lives. Divine Origin enlightens the mind with the Knowledge of the Being as Source, the 'becoming of appearances' and the returning into Being. This Divine Form becomes the basis for contemplating the Natural Mind, the origin or Source as the foundation of all mind processes, and the possibility to transcend and liberate all karma or subjective processes into the Calm–abiding State of the objective Natural Mind or Divine Origin.

Divine Origin is suspended from the Super Form of the Good Man or the virtue of Spirit, the Transcendental Good, which makes human beings become The Good in the sense of becoming divinized in themselves or attaining divinity by the force of the grace pouring from the Super Form of Divine Good. In the trinitarian dynamics of the Living Group, Divine Origin is the second moment, that of *reaction,* and receives the power of Divine Will, which is the *action* (proceeding) moment. Divine Will, with its internal Absolute Freedom, is its own *reaction* (returning) into Divine Origin; it is the fulfillment of Divine Will in the 'process of becoming' fully enlightened by the fullness of the Pleroma of the Divine Forms. Divine Origin, because it belongs to the triad of the Living Group, has as its fundamental intention that which is concerned with a Divine Humanity. As the Being Group is concerned with the Divine Being of God and the Doing Group is concerned with the Divine Spirit of Knowledge or Divine Gnosis, the triad of the Living Group has as its *function* the divinity of man by means of the Supreme Virtues, by which the process of the divinization of human beings actually happens. The Divine Trinity of the Ancients—which appears in the great Sumerian Trinity of Anu, God the Father; Enlil, the Divine Logos and Creator; and the Great Mother Ishtar as the Providential Spirit of God—was repeated in the Babylonian, Assyrian and Olympian myths with a common conception of three different consecutive creations. The Egyptian Trinity from Heliopolis was composed of the Absolute God, Atum, the Primordial One who is absolutely transcendent and uncreated; the god Shu; and the goddess Tefnut. Shu is Atum's son and the Creator of life and the Word of God in the form of Divine Air or Sound or the Divine Breath of Life; and Tefnut was the Divine Spirit, who preserves everything under the image of life–sustaining Spirit. All three were of one substance. This Egyptian Trinity reappears in the Eleusinian Mysteries with the trinity of Demeter, Persephone and the incarnated god Dionysius, as the fountain of salvation and immortality. Plato also posits a similar trinity with the Absolute Good as the Father, the Divine Demiurge as the Creator, and Moira as Divine Destiny of the Spirit. A final and more perfected trinity is from the great Neoplatonist Plotinus who conceived the Divine Trinity with the first person being the One Transcendental Good, the second person as the *Nous* (Gk) or Divine Mind of Transcendental Forms, by which the Mind through its Word or Logos emanates the third person, the Soul or the Universal Spirit that permeates everything and appears in all human beings. Late in the fourth century AD, the Cappadocian Fathers furnished the Christian doctrines of the Holy Trinity for the first time; they were not completely accepted or finalized until late in the fifth century.

In the Enneagram of the Divine Forms, Divine Origin refers to the triad of the Living Group suspended by the Form of the Divine Man or the archetypal man, the Adam Kadmon of the Ancients. Thus, its metaphysical question is directed to the perfection of man, the Transcendental Divine Man, who exists as the Divine Human Prototype in the Unity of the Eternal Divine Trinity. Therefore, the search for the Divine Origin of humankind is a search for the authentic Divine Essence of man, and this cannot be any other than the Divine Nature of 'humankind in itself.' This Innate Awareness is felt as life and existence and as being primordially a Mind that has been awakened into the Light of its own consciousness in the form of a transparency which is such because it is empty of relative conceptions. Thus, we arrive at Divine Origin, which is our own nature or the ground of our Mind in a pre–thinking State or a pre–logical State without the duality that is inseparable from any thinking process. In order to attain this situation of entering into our Source and Divine Origin, Divine Will and Freedom have to be attained. For only while entering into the perfect peace of the True Light of the Spirit will we be able to abide in our Divine Origin, which transcends time and space, and which is the nature of immortality.

MENTATIONAL ANALYSIS OF DIVINE ORIGIN

1 **SUBSTANCE** (What is it?) Divine Origin is the source of the *action* (proceeding) moment and the *reaction* (returning) of the being and the becoming (realization of potentialities).

2 **FORM** (How is it?) The Form of Divine Origin has its form in the Universal Form/Idea that there is nothing in the Universe without a cause or an origin.

3 **POSSIBILITIES** (Why originated?) Divine Origin is the insight that the Source and the process are one and the same.

4 **NEEDS** (What purpose?) Divine Origin is the manifestation of the Divine Will of Creation.

5 **IMPULSE** (What intention?) Divine Origin unites the Will and the Harmony of the 'process of being and becoming.'

6 **METHOD** (How accomplished?) Divine Origin is the contemplation of Ultimate Reality, where the natural State of Mind is found while abiding in a Mind of Non–duality.

7 **STANDARD** (What is the ideal?) Divine Origin, as the Source of all appearances, is the standard of being beyond duality.

8 **ORIENTATION** (What is the direction?) Divine Origin, as the Source, gives direction toward the completion of the process in the Source or the Natural Mind of Non–duality.

9 **CAPACITY** (What is the strength?) The strength of Divine Origin is in its permanency and completeness, because as a constant Source of the Good Man, it becomes an inexhaustible fountain of the presence of the Natural Mind of harmonious Unity.

10 **CHARISMA** (What is the appearance?) Divine Ori-

gin is presented to us as a vision of the Pure Light which arises as a golden–green–violet Light of Divine Presence.

11 **MEANS** (How produced?) By means of acquiring a Pure Mind beyond karma and dispositions of suffering, it is possible to return to the innocence of the Form of Divine Origin.

12 **GOALS** (What is attained?) With the Form of Divine Origin, we attain a true and indispensable guide toward the realization and completion of returning to the Source.

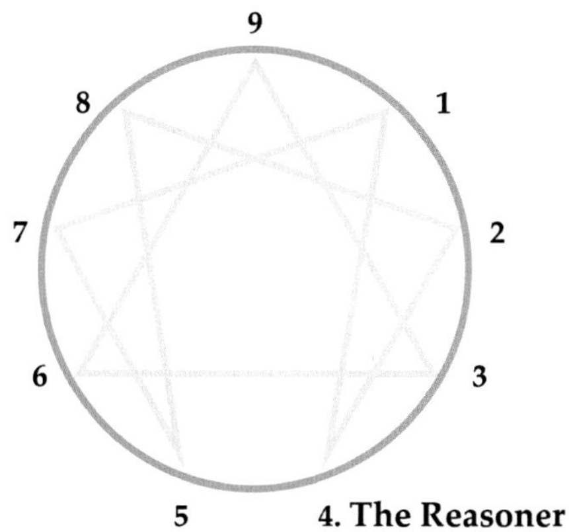

THE FIXATION OF THE REASONER

The Form of Divine Origin corresponds in the Enneagram of the Fixations to the fixated point 4 of the Reasoner. All the names of the Ego–Fixations in Protoanalysis have the particular connotation of not being authentic in themselves, but are rather an over–exaggeration that makes them appear out of place and in the attitude of a clown lost in the middle of the circus, tumbling with no direction. Reasoners, because they lack Divine Origin, seriously do not know what they really are and, in this sense, they question everything with a constant "why," trying to find a cause or a purpose to their own life and everything else. This constant questioning makes the Reasoner always appear in a reflective manner, searching for origins and finalities in a way that can be trivial and annoying.

EGO–REDUCTION OF THE REASONER

The Living Group has as its Existential Attitudes Anger, Anxiety and a "chip on the shoulder" that appear in the Reasoner because of their imagined projection of being painfully criticized by their father figure, provoking anxiety in them and giving this Fixation the ego–delusion of living in a state of Melancholia; they appear to be yearning for approval. The Passion of the Reasoner is Envy and wanting to be one of those who succeed and receive the approval of others. Their Dichotomy on one side is Argumentative and on the other Superficial. The Primary Defense Mechanism of the Reasoner is based on Sublimation or behavior by which unacceptable drives are diverted into manifestations that are socially acceptable. For instance, instead of provoking a confrontation, angry and violent urges may be diverted into physical activity or misappropriated as God's Will. The ego–position is Self–justification because of their constant thinking and reasoning about life. The ego–balancer for the Reasoner is "I am reasonable and informed." The difficulty is being ashamed of themselves. Their ego–reaction is to be discouraged by the critical attitude of others and the world. The Reasoner's ego–justification is being apprehensive about life. They use the Door of Compensation of Crime in the sense of deceptively living with certain aspects of corruption. The Dichotomic Existential Attitudes of the Reasoner are Easygoing on one side and Intolerant on the other. Their way out is through Clarity of thought without ambivalence, and this leads to the Fixation's Trap (Authenticity), which will open the Form of Divine Origin and reduce the Ego–Fixation of the Reasoner and its process.

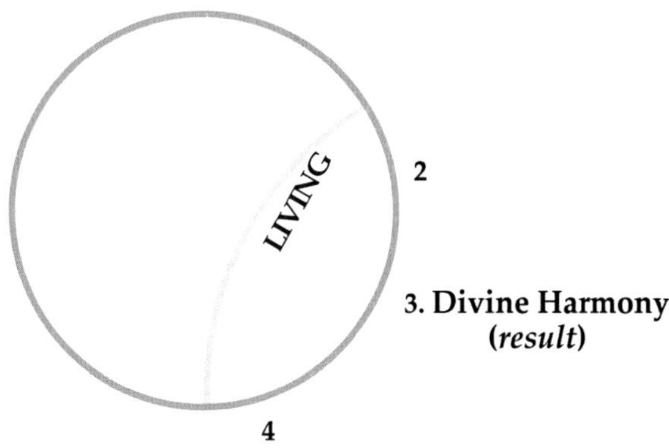

DIVINE HARMONY (Point 3)

In the triad of the Living Group, the Form of Divine Harmony is the *resulting* (sustaining) point. It has a particular strength because it is the pivotal point, since in it the process of the Super Form of the Good Man, or The Good living in society, becomes completed and discovers and obtains the harmony between Being and the 'process of becoming.' This is to say, a harmony exists between the Creator with His Creation by way of Providential Laws which sustain the continuous process of Creation by way of a flow, a movement, or a force that develops itself between pre–established points of manifestation (first Law of Trialectics), where every point of manifestation has in itself an active triad that develops an internal triadic movement (second Law of Trialectics); and this flow is cyclical with a descending and an ascending movement by virtue of the attraction of the primordial point that closes the cycle (third Law of Trialectics).

The most fundamental Laws of the objective world are known as the Law of Three and the Law of Seven of the *Chaldean Oracles,* and as the Law of the Ennead of the Neoplatonists. By knowing these Laws, we can condition ourselves, so to speak, with a harmonious flow of Divine Reality which appears as moving, not at random or accidentally, but moving from one level of manifestation to a higher one. When the series of steps are completed, one cycle is over and a new one begins, exactly upon the same pattern. This indispensable Knowledge of the steps of every process gives us the power to analyze and understand situations, events, people, and our life as a whole. This Knowledge of process is as indispensable in our spiritual search and understanding as the knowledge of the pre–established patterns of the seasons is for agriculture, animal breeding, and hunting. Equally indispensable is the proper Knowledge of the Law of Three or the Law of the Triad which, as referred to before, is analyzed by the Neoplatonists as proceeding, returning and sustaining; and by Trialectics as *action, reaction* and *result.* These three moments are sustained or supported by a super moment that is the cause and the goal of the triad, known as the "function." In the triad of the Living Group of the Divine Forms, the *function* of the triad is the Super Form of the Good Person or the 'good life.' When reality is understood by way of these two supreme Laws (Law of Three and Law of Seven), the entire reality becomes spiritualized because we come to discover that it is alive and it has a purpose in the sense that it is a pre–established reality or that it has been designed purposefully and thus, teleologically by a Divine Agent. This Knowledge opens the understanding of the Form of Divine Will or what we can call the Divine Purpose of The Good. When we understand this point, we really come to see The Good and the perfection in nature and then, as a reflection, The Good and the Perfection in ourselves, in our Transcendental Self, and in that which can understand the Divine Laws that support the Divine Providence or Divine Will.

Acquiring the fullness of Divine Harmony by enlightening our Mind with the Divine Forms is necessary in the process because, by understanding the Laws of Harmony or the Trialectical Laws, we enter into an objective view of reality, where we can abstract and understand the Laws of Nature, such as the Newtonian Law of Gravitation, because the internal Laws of the 'process of becoming' have to actually be discovered in all our environment, externally in nature and society and internally in our biological and psychical processes. This is to say that by situating a process in the right step, we know immediately and exactly what to expect from that point in the process. For instance, if we are observing the process of life, we know exactly what it is to be a child and what to expect from childhood. This very obvious observation, when it is related to a complete pattern, can be seen from the point of the process as a function of the Totality and thus, it will make sense of the coherent and harmonic developments of all reality. Having this view is important because it produces in us the realization that there is a flow of the 'process of becoming,' which can actually be visualized in the form of a liquid Light or the "spiritual water" of the Ancients that appears to flow through all reality. Having this view of reality, in accordance with the harmonic Trialectical Laws, we attain an insight into Reality as it really is, beyond simple intellection, the thinking and rationalizing with which we fall into the schema of duality and by that into a world view that is subjective and egocentric.

Divine Harmony is envisioned as the manifestation of the Being in the 'process of becoming'; it does not disintegrate in the 'process of becoming' but is sustained in its Totality by the Laws of Divine Harmony, which are the constant manifestation of the Unity of the entire Cosmos as one Eternal process of the One Eternal Creator, both being One and inseparable. Thus, Being and becoming are found to be one and the same. When we attain this view, we look at Reality as it really is, in its transcendentality in the sense that the sustaining Harmonic Laws are in themselves permanent, pre–established and Eternal, and it is these Laws that equate with the One Being, which is permanent, Eternal and Unchangeable. If we come to sustain the view of Divine Harmony, we enter into a State of constant Self–awareness because we have become the objective point of view of Divine Harmony. When this happens, real hope arises, but here it is not a wishful type of hope that belongs to the correlative Ego–Fixation of the Displayer, but is a hope that the Laws of Divine Harmony are conducive to the realization of the Supreme Hope of attaining total Enlightenment and transcendentality in our spiritual realization.

The Form of Divine Harmony was central to the Pythagoreans because they discovered that reality starts from the most ethereal manifestation in the form of sound, which is a vibration that can be measured, and Pythagoras discovered that there was a mathematical ratio between the length of the matter and the sound that could be produced. Furthermore, these ratios could be found in the relationships between the first four digits, and they could be ordered in a triangular form using dots to obtain with precision the ratios as well as the sum of ten, which was considered the perfect number. The discovery that the Laws of reality are expressions of a harmonious relation and thus, intrinsically Good and intrinsically Providential shows the Infinite Wisdom of the Designer of such a Cosmos, where all is in the State of Harmony. This contemplation of the Divine of all was the Transcendental Knowledge of the Pythagoreans, a special type of Knowledge, a Gnosis, which alone can penetrate and understand that which is Universal, Infinite and Absolute. This view penetrates with a profound insight into all nature; by finding its Supreme Harmony, we come to understand and appreciate the infinite beauty of a Creation that is The Beautiful because it is harmonious and perfect.

The Divine Harmony of the Cosmos, the central theme of Plato's *Timaeus* and the Divine Demiurge, who was Good, creates the Cosmos upon the models of the Divine Forms; and everything proceeds in that order, but it does so because the Cosmos is founded upon numbers which in themselves mean harmonies that are the structure of all and, consequently, the basic and only true Reality. Chaos is considered a disharmony and lacks the structure of numbers. The same 'doctrine of

Harmonious Providence' and its inner sense of a harmonious life—where all the elements coincide in the patterns of related harmony—produce the Mind of the Sage or the Wise Man, who could look at reality the way that it really is because they could understand its harmony and beauty directly, and they would live their lives producing only appropriate actions, or those infused by a Mind that has transcended the mental process produced by the appearances of reality or the *phantasia* (Gk) of imagined phenomenon. The Sage could paralyze or grasp the Totality of the Mind and open the Mind of Silence and Transcendentality in what the Stoics called *kataleptike phantasia* (Gk), which would produce appropriate actions—harmonious acts that the Stoics called *kathekonta* (Gk). We can say that all Neoplatonism is the study of harmony in relation to cosmology and the theogony or the Creation of the Cosmos and the gods.

From this point comes the theory and the doctrines of emanation by which are produced in succession the three Creations. The first Creation corresponds to the 'Absolute Divine in itself' in the form of a triad of Gods of the Divine Spheres, the three of them being of the same substance, which is the Divine Triad or the Godhead. The second Creation corresponds to the world of Forms or the world of the *Nous* of the Neoplatonists, which was preceded by the Supreme Creator, the Divine Demiurge who in Neoplatonic texts is the Supreme God Zeus, who presides over the mental spheres. The third Creation is of the younger gods who produce the Souls and the psychic spheres. Beyond these spheres is the material sphere of the sub–lunar elements. This schema shows the related harmony between the three triads that make the ennead of gods, plus the material sphere which together makes ten, the perfect number of the Pythagoreans. The Sumerian cosmo-theogony, with its three Creations with their ennead of gods, is parallel to the Egyptian ennead of Hermopolis and to the Ancient Greek model of Orphic theogony and the Eleusinian, as well as the Samothracian mysteries, which are basically followed by the Neoplatonic schema with the ladder of emanated spheres, which were also known as attributes of the Supreme. The Neoplatonic schema passed into the Western world by way of the Christian Neoplatonists Pseudo–Dionysius, Erigena, Jakob Boehme, and Leibniz; the Romantic Philosophers Fichte, Schelling and Hegel; and more recently in the 1920s, Samuel Alexander and Alfred North Whitehead, known to contemporary scholarship as the "Process Philosophers." Thus, the influence of Divine Harmony appears upon reality in accordance with a perfect and harmonic schema, which can be contemplated in such a way that we can come to hear the Divine Harmonies or have the perfect ecstatic transcendence of a vision by which we acquire the understanding of the whole and the opening into the Super Form of the Unity of God.

MENTATIONAL ANALYSIS OF DIVINE HARMONY

1. **SUBSTANCE** (What is it?) The Laws of Divine Harmony are the providential Perfection of the Being in the Eternal flow of the Cosmos.
2. **FORM** (How is it?) Divine Harmony manifests by the Laws of Seven, Three and Cycles.
3. **POSSIBILITIES** (How originated?) The Laws of Divine

Harmony have their origin as the pre–established Laws of the Source or the Being.

4 **NEEDS** (What purpose?) Divine Harmony sustains the Unity of the entire Cosmos as one single process.

5 **IMPULSE** (What intention?) With Divine Harmony, we can objectively observe Reality as it is, and by this view we acquire the experience and transcendentality of the dialectical Laws.

6 **METHOD** (How accomplished?) By the view of reality as it is, we produce a constant Innate Awareness that is objective and independent, which constantly increases our realization of the Pure Light of Consciousness.

7 **STANDARD** (What is the ideal?) Divine Harmony means to have certainty in the applicability of the Divine Laws, producing in us real and complete hope.

8 **ORIENTATION** (What is the direction?) Divine Harmony, once we are aware of it, because it is the function of the flow of Reality, allows us to hope with certainty for a continuous and not declining constant spiritual Work and internal Realization.

9 **CAPACITY** (What is the strength?) Divine Harmony has the ability to sustain the Work of spiritual Realization in a natural and constant flow across Divine Will and Divine Origin.

10 **CHARISMA** (What is the appearance?) Divine Harmony gives a profound sense of security about The Good of all Creation and a sense of peace in the confidence of The Good or what is harmonious and perfect.

11 **MEANS** (How produced?) The Form of Divine Harmony is produced by the recognition of the three Trialectical Laws of Objective Reality.

12 **GOALS** (What is attained?) With Divine Harmony, it is possible to attain the peace of certainty and a contemplation of Reality and the Light of Consciousness in a constant Unity and inseparability.

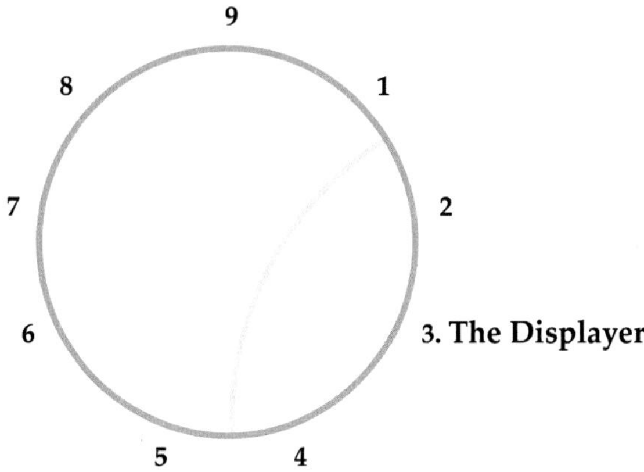

THE FIXATION OF THE DISPLAYER

The fixated point 3 of the Displayer is the obscuration of the Form of Divine Harmony, which opens us to the perfect Reality. The main characteristic of the Displayer is that, because they are ignorant of the Laws of Divine Harmony, they cannot observe or appreciate the perfection of the Cosmos and instead react by developing their own sense of perfection and harmony. In this way, they separate themselves from the harmonious flow of Reality and become the creators of their own reality, a reality that is in complete disharmony, repetitious, cacophonic, and strident. The Displayer has the ego–delusion of being an extraordinary doer and performer of acts of great display and flamboyance. But the Laws of the Form of Divine

Harmony mean Divine Hope in the sense of certitude of The Good flowing through everything, instead of the Displayer's complete uncertainty and discomfort of being inadequate, with the intense anxiety and anger of not being good enough.

The Ego–Fixation is an actual obscuration behind which the Divine Form abides in its perfect and Eternal Form, but the Divine Form is obscured to us because of the intense attention that we give to a certain point where our emotions are particularly affected by the natural process of our living. The 'Ego–Fixation in itself' accumulates other layers by which the Divine Form is also covered, making it even more impenetrable. This successive covering, like the ever–building layers of a shell, has to be dismantled or broken down one by one in a process of ego–reduction or the deconstruction of these successive layers of ego–residue, with its fourteen layers from the Ego–Fixation to the Divine Form.

EGO–REDUCTION OF THE DISPLAYER

The Ego–Fixation of Displayers is formed by their projection of being ignored by their father, which provokes desire in them and produces the Existential Attitudes of anger and anxiety that give them an attitude of having a "chip on their shoulder." The ego–delusion of the Displayer is Vanity because of their terror of being ignored, which makes them "Go for it, take charge, and present yourself with all you've got." Their Passion is Deceit in the sense of make–believe as in professional acting, the political arena, or the military display of action. The Dichotomy appears as Cunning and efficient on one side and Bluffing and histrionic on the other. The Displayer has the Primary

Defense Mechanism of Identification with their own conduct and social theater wherein they assume identities by imitating another person or fictional character imagined as a role model, or they identify with the values and attitudes of a group. Their ego–position is that of Self–deception. The Displayer uses the ego–balancer "I am practiced and innovative." The Displayer's difficulty is their terror of being unconvincing. Their ego–reaction is the extreme anguish they experience for appearing inauthentic. The Displayer's ego–justification for any mistake or blunder is to complain and project blame on others. They use the Door of Compensation of Over–exertion as their way to pacify themselves for their lack of results and success. The Displayer's Dichotomic Existential Attitudes are being Authentic on one side and Theatrical on the other. The way out for the Displayer is their Creativity, which will lead them to their Trap—to be efficient and harmonious. It is through this Trap that the Displayer can enter into the Form of Divine Harmony which will dissolve their Fixation.

CHAPTER 4

THE DOING GROUP

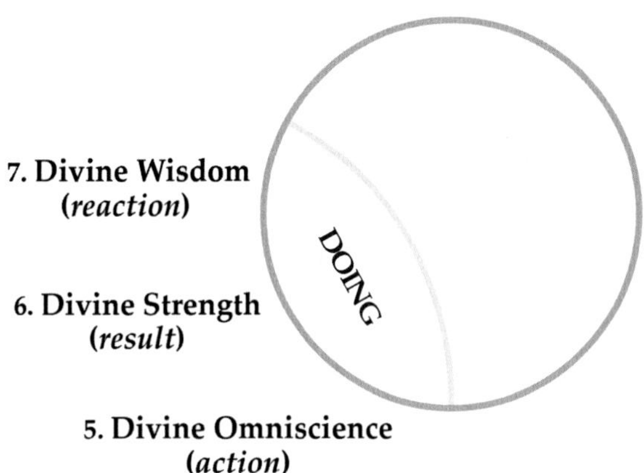

TRIAD OF THE DOING GROUP

The Enneagram of the Fixations of the Existential Mind (Sphere 15) is composed of the three triads of the Being, Living and Doing Groups that are suspended from the three Instincts, which are the *functions* of their corresponding triad. The Doing Group corresponds to the Adaptation Instinct—how we adapt ourselves to the environment and, further on by way of working with utensils and technology, how we have come to adapt the environment to our own needs of survival. The Conservation Instinct is concerned with being and 'existence in itself.' The Relation Instinct is concerned with living in a community, and for this purpose our ability to communicate and interrelate with other human beings is essential in order to make our survival possible. The Adaptation Instinct is concerned with doing and the knowledge of how to actually do something in the sense of adapting that something to our own purposes.

Thus, the Doing Group is the constant general awareness of how to survive through adaptation. The Ego – Fixations connected to the Doing Group are the Observer (point 5), which is the point of *action* (proceeding); the Idealist (point 7), which is the *reaction* (returning) point; and the Adventurer (point 6), which is the *result* (sustaining). In the corresponding Enneagram of the Divine Forms of the Creative Mind (Sphere 7), the Doing Group is composed of Divine Omniscience (point 5) which is the *action* (proceeding) point; Divine Wisdom (point 7) which is the *reaction* (returning) point; and Divine Strength (point 6) which is the *result* (sustaining). Each triad is concerned with one of three main realms of the philosophical investigation that answer the three fundamental questions of "What is being?" or the questions of ontology; "What is the Good Man?" or the questions of ethics; and "What is the Universal Spirit?" or the questions of metaphysics.

Thus, specifically, the triad of the Doing Group is suspended from the Super Form of the Universal Spirit which becomes the *function* of the triad of the Doing Group. This Super Form of the Universal Spirit can also be said to be the Ultimate Goal of survival through the Adaptation Instinct into the Divine Forms of faith and immortality, as the supreme sense of survival. Thus, the metaphysical questions about Supreme Knowledge or Omniscience (point 5), perfect Wisdom (point 7), and total faith or Strength (point 6) support us to persevere in spiritual practices or direct Work with the Divine. Again, we have to see that the Super Forms generate the super energy necessary for being the *function* of the given triad. Thus, the realm of the Super Form of Being is energized by the Super Form of Divine Compassion. The Super Form of the Divine Good Man promotes the energy of Divine Hope, and the Super Form of Universal Spirit produces the energy of Divine Faith. The three Super Forms, when seen as a trinity, reflect the trinitarian structure of the Godhead. This is to say that these Super Forms are the core of the theological understanding of the Enneagram of the Nine Divine Forms.

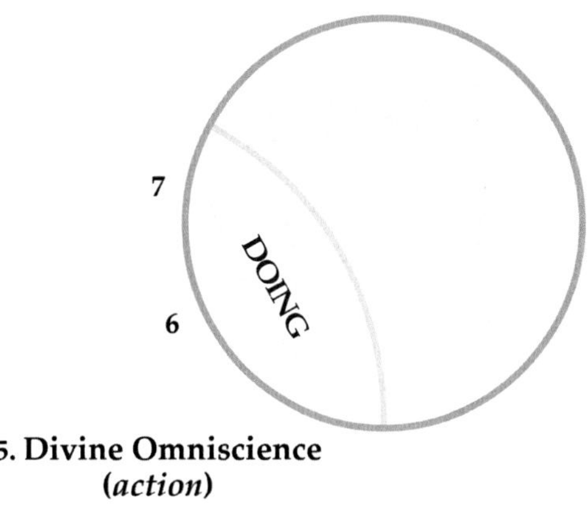

5. Divine Omniscience
(*action*)

DIVINE OMNISCIENCE (Point 5)

Divine Omniscience is the *action* point (proceeding) of the triad of the Doing Group. In the triad of the Being Group, the Super Form and the *function* is the Being or God, and in the triad of the Living Group, the Super Form and *function* is the Good Man or the Divine Man. The triad of the Doing Group has, as its Super Form and *function*, the Universal Spirit that contains and supports everything. The Being and Living Groups answer ontological and ethical questions respectively; the questions in the Doing Group are metaphysical and refer to the Ultimate Reality as Knowledge itself, as the third triadic element in the super triad of God (Being), The Good (Living), and Knowledge or Gnosis (Doing). Thus the Doing Group becomes suspended from the Super Form of the Universal Spirit which is essentially Gnosis or Pure Consciousness, Perfect Innate Awareness, with the insight and understanding of the timeless Presence of that immediate Knowledge that can have a view of the Totality or a view of the completeness of 'Mind in itself,' a Mind that has itself as its object, which can look at itself as in a clear reflection. This Mind that contemplates without the interference of thought and duality understands that, in fact, the Universal Spirit is everything; and, even more important, the Universal Spirit is consciousness which is equated with the Absolute Knowledge that is the understanding that everything is Consciousness or the Mind awakened to the reality that there is only Mind or Divine Gnosis.

This insight that in the final analysis Ultimate Reality is Gnosis or the Mind in its Pure Essence which is perfect and complete, opens the Form of Divine Omniscience. Thus, Divine Omniscience is not something to be attained since it is the basis of all Knowledge; it is transcendental to ordinary comprehension and requires a Higher State of Innate Awareness, as do all the Divine Forms. As we have seen, we are required to open the ninth Sphere of the Enlightened Mind, where the Light is produced by the union of the Absolute and Relative Minds, giving rise to the Mind of Light or the Ornamental Mind. With this Mind of Pure Innate Awareness, we become permeated and completely absorbed with the Universal and complete Knowledge of Divine Omniscience, which is an unmediated and timeless Gnosis. Thus, Divine Omniscience is not something to be learned, but to be suddenly completed and perfected by it by being permeated and absorbed in it. Therefore, Divine Omniscience gives us an insight into the Unity of all cosmic processes. This Unity is based on the fact that everything in the Cosmos is interdependent and consequently relative. When, by this insight of Divine Omniscience, we discover that everything that is an appearance is also relative and interdependent, we can see the Mind of Divine Omniscience as the absolute basis upon which all relative appearances are actually founded.

Thus, the Form of Divine Omniscience, as the *action* (proceeding) moment in the triad of the Doing Group, suspended from the Super Form of Divine Gnosis or the Divine Presence of the Spirit, is in the Form of a pure, uncontaminated Innate Awareness. When we perceive this Pure Innate Awareness or Gnosis, we can see in front of us that liquid transparency clothed with incredibly subtle colors as mist. Our State of Innate Awareness or this Living Gnosis is Pure Spirit and Pure Consciousness. This is what we have to understand when we study Divine Omniscience, which is the *action* (proceeding) moment of the triad of the Doing Group, whose *function* or Ultimate Purpose is Divine Gnosis. Thus, Divine Omniscience points to the universality of Divine Gnosis. Divine Gnosis is the Universal Spirit of God or the Holy Spirit that is essentially consciousness, bliss and Light. Divine Omniscience is the attribute of Divine Gnosis being universally present.

We first find the 'doctrine of Divine Omniscience' in Anaximander's proposition that the Ultimate Reality or physis, wrongly translated as matter, was the *apeiron* (Gk), the

Boundless, which is undifferentiated stuff. From this point, he established that the present state of the Universe, with its extremely complex structure of matter, in fact evolved from a primordial condition of simplicity. The Boundless was infinite in extent and infinite in time, since it was conceived as ageless and deathless. In the fifth century BC, Anaxagoras taught in Athens that 'all is mind,' in itself absolutely pure, containing no mixture. But nevertheless, it was fundamentally Consciousness, and it did not rule the Universe in any way or any sense, because of its own Essential Nature of being pure and unmixed. We know that Socrates became disillusioned with the mind proposed by Anaxagoras because, in the last analysis, this mind was not even a Demiurge, since this mind could not create anything and thus, there was no possibility of worshipping the mind, since it was unreachable and unknowable. But Anaxagoras was speaking of the Mind that essentially is the Pristine Awareness of Consciousness. Aristotle in his description of human intelligence affirmed that the Intelligence was only One, complete and perfect. This produced one of the biggest controversies in the history of philosophy.

During the twelfth century AD, the Arab culture poured into Europe through Spain and brought with it the Arabic translations of Aristotle, plus the commentaries of the great Arab philosophers and the works of the Spaniard Averroes, who with Avicenna were fundamental and essential for establishing the Scholastic philosophy that was based mainly on Aristotle. The highest representative of the Christian Tradition was Thomas Aquinas who absorbed all of Aristotle with very few reinterpretations or alterations, except for the Aristotelian theory that the Intellect is one and the same everywhere and in everybody, since to Aquinas this apparently broke the necessary barriers of the individual. This, of course, is misunderstanding Intelligence as being reason and there does not seem to be any objection that Aquinas considered Intelligence in this sense, because Aristotle himself recognized reasoning as the highest function in a human being. But we have to remember that for Aristotle, the Intellect had two different modes. One he called the "first entelechy," which was transcendent, absolute and capable of contemplating the Divine Forms (Ideas) which were simple and uniform. Because of this simplicity in the sense of 'Mind in itself' without content, a Pure Mind, it has to be one and the same everywhere and in every human being, and because the quality of this Mind or first entelechy is its transcendence and Eternity, Aristotle insisted that this was the only part of a human being that would not die because it has the quality of immortality. The second part or mode of Aristotle's Intellect was called the "second entelechy" and, as the functions of the first entelechy were absorption, contemplation, intuition, and vision, the functions of the second entelechy were reason, understanding, memory, and imagination.

We can see that Aquinas understood Aristotle only partially, and took the second entelechy as being the only intelligence of human beings. This misunderstanding of Aristotle had enormous consequences because it denies any possibility of a mystical way toward Union with the Divine, and this perceptible lacuna in Aquinas' philosophy and theology was acutely felt by the followers of the philosophy of St. Augustine, who adhered to the Platonic contemplation of Ideas and, as the

Neoplatonists are quick to point out, Aristotle adhered and was loyal to this Platonic 'doctrine of contemplation.' Quite dramatically the Franciscan Order opposed the Aristotelianism of Aquinas. St. Bonaventure, the head of the Franciscan Order, went so far as to point out that such a doctrine was just materialistic, and in his *The Journey of the Mind into God,* he analyzes this journey in six stages of ascension which remind us quite vividly of the Neoplatonism of Scotus Erigena and the Platonic School of Chartres. But regardless of the unpopularity of Aquinas in his own time, three hundred years later in the Council of Trent, and with the influence of the Jesuits, this incomplete Aristotelianism of Aquinas was imposed as the official doctrine of the Church. However, it also influenced Descartes and the Rationalists, who understood Intelligence as being equivalent to reason and thus, the failure of Aquinas's rationalistic taking of the mind was corrected by the critical philosophy of Kant, which reestablished the transcendent Intellect that he calls "*noumena.*"

Therefore, this Aristotelian first entelechy—a Mind of contemplation, intuition and vision, and which in Integral Philosophy is the Absolute Mind—has Divine Omniscience as its *action* (proceeding). Because of the qualities we have observed of singularity and homogeneity that make it Universal, ever-present and unchanging Pure Mind, Divine Omniscience posits the Truth that by necessity, when we enter into true Gnosis, we acquire Divine Omniscience. By knowing the simplicity and universality of Divine Gnosis, we know instantly that that Mind in us is exactly the same in every human being and throughout the Universe as the Divine Spirit of God, which is

Pure Consciousness and Gnosis. It also means that we perceive through Divine Omniscience the Divine Human Prototype (the State of the Eternal Presence), which abides in the center of the heart, and which is one and the same in every human being.

Divine Omniscience, as the *action* (proceeding) aspect of the triad of the Doing Group, has the force of contemplating and understanding 'wholes' or Totalities which, because of their completeness, produce the first omniscience or the sense of Totality and the Innate Awareness of Unity, which any Totality or whole demands. There is the omniscient Knowledge of the Absolute One, whose Totality cannot be questioned, because to do so would be logically contradictory. Then there is the Totality of the Cosmos which is ultimately based in the Divine Spirit or Divine Consciousness. When we arrive at the total understanding of the Divine Spirit as the Ultimate Reality, we enter into the second Divine Omniscience that understands the Totality of the Universal Spirit. A third omniscience is developed by the understanding that the pattern of the Universe is the Universal Man, the microcosm, and that all human beings have in themselves a Divine Spark, from which the Universal Divine Human Prototype is realized in its Perfection and Totality. These are the only three Totalities or independent 'wholes,' which are discovered by Divine Omniscience. It is in Divine Wisdom where the three omnisciences will demand their Unity in order to attain the Ultimate Oneness of all, which means to enter into the Mind of God and to arrive into True Enlightenment.

MENTATIONAL ANALYSIS OF DIVINE OMNISCIENCE

1 **SUBSTANCE** (What is it?) Divine Omniscience is the Infinite Innate Awareness of Consciousness as transparent infinite space.

2 **FORM** (How is it?) Divine Omniscience is the transparency of Innate Awareness beyond duality and judgment.

3 **POSSIBILITIES** (Why originated?) Divine Omniscience is the manifestation of Universal Knowledge and Spirit or Gnosis.

4 **NEEDS** (What purpose?) Divine Omniscience is the awakening into The State of complete certitude that 'All is Mind.'

5 **IMPULSE** (What intention?) Divine Omniscience is the constant recovery of the transparency of Pure Innate Awareness. When we enter into this State, we have the beyond normal perception that we ourselves, especially our Mind, have become transparent and we have become invisible.

6 **METHOD** (How accomplished?) Divine Omniscience is reproduced by perceiving the unmediated Knowledge or Gnosis.

7 **STANDARD** (What is the ideal?) Divine Omniscience gives us the timeless Knowledge of the presence of the Universal Spirit.

8 **ORIENTATION** (What is the direction?) Divine Omniscience opens the Innate Awareness of the Unity of all processes into the Ornamental Mind.

9 **CAPACITY** (What is the strength?) Divine Omniscience

is the Universal and complete Knowledge of Transcendental Innate Awareness.

10 **CHARISMA** (What is the appearance?) Divine Omniscience is visualized as brilliant green in the Innate Light of the Mind.

11 **MEANS** (How produced?) Divine Omniscience appears and is opened by direct insight into the nature of the Mind.

12 **GOALS** (What is attained?) Divine Omniscience reveals itself as the transparent Innate Awareness of the Pure Light.

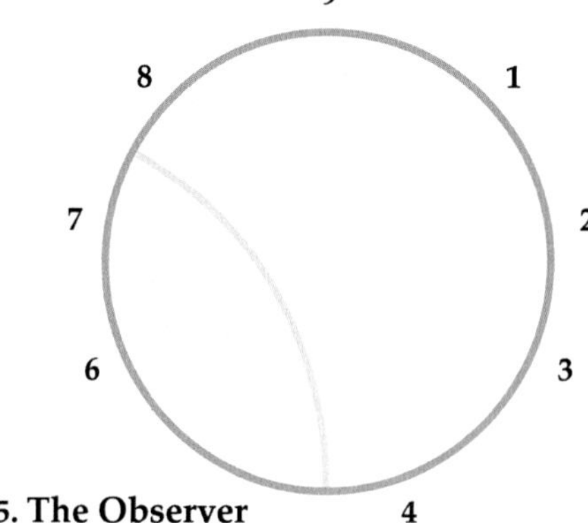

THE FIXATION OF THE OBSERVER

The fixated point 5 of the Observer means that, by the Laws of the Form of Divine Omniscience, we have lost that vast openness of Mind that is felt as pure transparency in an open space. This Innate Awareness is Universal and without any relative content of conceptual thinking and language; when lost, the Universal point of view is also lost, and so we lose the conception that all appearances are interrelated and relative. Instead, the fixated point of the Observer will narrow the Universal view of Divine Omniscience into the particular and subjective point of view of the Observer. Because of their lack of Divine Omniscience, they do not have a Universal and objective point of view, because omniscience means the Knowledge of 'wholes' and an all–encompassing view that produces Transcendence and insight into Ultimate Reality. Thus, the Observer is always losing perspective of the forest because their entire attention is on particular trees. Therefore, the Observer is found collecting bits and pieces and can spend a lot of time trying to disclose the riddles of life and society. Because of their continuous interest in observing others, they fear that they are also the focus of attentive study and observation by others, which makes them inclined to hide and be anonymous around people. Their general inclination is to play the social game without giving of themselves completely and openly.

In the correlative Enneagram of the Fixations of the Existential Mind (Sphere 15), the triad of the Doing Group is suspended from the Adaptation Instinct, which is concerned with the knowledge of how to adapt our environment, natural and social, in order to make our survival possible. Thus, the doing aspect of the Instinct is intimately connected with know–how at every level of activity. The Conservation Instinct is concerned with the entire body, as existence and being, and the Relation Instinct is mainly preoccupied with emotions that provide the most straightforward communications and relations in a human society. The Adaptation Instinct is interested in the knowledge of the environment, natural and social, and how to work with it and produce and do things by working with nature or the given society. The Adaptation Instinct becomes deeply influenced by the Polar Preconception of fighting a war against a forbidding, cruel and deceitful world. This affects the Adaptation Instinct by charging it with a sense of warfare and of conquering, by way of aggression or attraction in the male/female modes. This appears in the Instinct as the Existential Attitudes of fear of the environment, natural and social, and as a constant stress, making the characteristics of the Doing Group manifest as people who could be called "nervous wrecks" because of the pressure of their fear and stress. As we have seen, those in the Being Group can be described as having a "broken heart" with the Existential Attitudes of sadness and depression, and those in the Living Group can be characterized as having a "chip on the shoulder" with the Existential Attitudes of anger and anxiety.

EGO–REDUCTION OF THE OBSERVER

The Observer perceives and projects their distortion of reality by thinking that they have been alienated by their siblings or the world, which distracts them and opens in their process the Existential Attitudes of Fear and Stress that make them appear as "nervous wrecks." Their ego–delusion is that of being Stingy or a person who keeps to themselves as they judge others exclusively from their personal perception and narrow point of view. The Observer has the Passion of Avarice; they amass information and accumulate pieces of knowledge and gossip about others, as well as collecting material things. Their Dichotomy is Meddling on one side and being Antisocial on the other. The Primary Defense Mechanism of the Observer is

Introjection in which they absorb themselves in and internalize the attributes and personalities of others by assimilating their behavior, emotions or characteristics as a coping mechanism. Their ego–position is being Self–obsessed, making them see themselves as a separate bystander. They use the ego–balancer of "I am sociable and self–sufficient" in order to deal with their given reality. The Observer's difficulty is their shyness which makes them nervous socially. Their main ego–reaction is one of distrust, which produces a constant looking in every direction. The Observer's ego–justification is to face facts with cynicism because of their poor idea of the motives and self–interest of others. The Door of Compensation that they use is Phobias, producing in themselves an intense aversion or a repulsion that is felt acutely, which becomes the starting point for their plotting and scheming. The Observer's Dichotomic Existential Attitude is that of being Considerate on one side and Imposing on the other. Their way out is to establish Agreement with themselves and the world, and this attitude will lead the Fixation into its own Trap, which is the keen Observation of all that happens to them. This observation will lead them to a profound State of Self–remembrance and with this State they will enter into the Form of Divine Omniscience that will give them the perspective to transcend their Fixation.

DIVINE WISDOM (Point 7)

Divine Wisdom is the *reaction* (returning) point of the triad of the Doing Group. It receives the Pure Innate Awareness of Divine Omniscience (point 5) and applies it as a Divine Plan to the *action* of Providential Wisdom. To absorb ourselves in Divine Wisdom, we have to surround ourselves with this

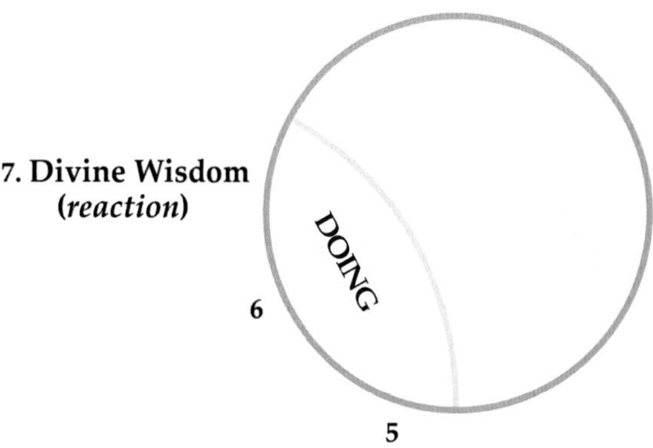

Divine Plan that is pre–established and already perfect. By this internal movement, it is possible to acquire the wisdom of not interfering with reality, which is known in ancient Taoism as *wu wei* (Chn) or the action of non–action, meaning the action that is spontaneous and appears naturally—not by prefabricated mental action.

The Form of Divine Wisdom is to live in a constant present State, since only what is present 'here and now' is Reality, and to live in the pure present of reality illuminates the purity of a Mind beyond judgment and the obscurations of duality and the reckoning of the facts. We have a further obscuration of our sense of Self that can appear only in a Mind of Perfect Presence of the 'here and now' of Divine Perfection, which reappears in Divine Wisdom, not as the perfection of Being, but as the point of view of that perfection. This Wisdom of pure Reality defines our sense of Being as Pure Presence. Heidegger, in his book *Being and Time,* analyzes temporality in its three moments of past, present and future, but finds that, because of our subjective processes, we are only living in the present by the knowledge and experiences of the past, which no longer exists, and we are also projecting ourselves to the future that does not yet exist, and in this way we forget that our real being can only be found by being in the present time. When we are living in this Pure Present, 'here and now,' a Mind of Pure Emptiness and Pure Light arises. By the specific Mind of being in the present, we can look at reality without the duality of like and dislike (Conservation), love and hate (Relation), or right and wrong (Adaptation). This view of Divine Wisdom is another aspect of Divine Gnosis (Higher Knowledge), which is the Super Form or the function of the triad of the Doing Group. Divine Wisdom, as the *reaction* aspect (returning) of the triad, naturally orients its energy of present Innate Awareness into point 6, Divine Strength, which is the actual consciousness and perception that the Supreme Spirit is 'Consciousness in itself' or Gnosis.

The Form of Divine Wisdom is the *reaction* (returning) moment of the triad of the Doing Group that is suspended and depends on the Super Form of Divine Knowledge. This is a Knowledge that is of a special kind, since it is a Knowledge that is not directed to knowing diverse objects and things of the external world or concepts and thoughts of the internal world, since this type of knowledge is knowledge about something in particular. But the specific Divine Knowledge that we are talking about is a Knowledge about the Ultimate Elements that form the Divine Triad of the Super Forms of God, the Absolute; the Good Man; and the Divine Spirit or Gnosis. This is a Knowledge that arises only when the three Super Forms have been made into one, known in the *philosophia perennis* (Lat) or Archaic Wisdom as the "process of the two becoming three."

This refers to the dynamics of the triads whose pattern, in fact, is the Divine Trinity of the Godhead. In these dynamics, the first two—God, the Absolute, and the Good Man or the Son—become united and together they produce the third person of the Trinity of the Spirit of God. This dynamic, of course, is simply a logically developed proposition, where there is an apparent precedence and a consequence. This cannot be so because the triple Divine Elements are co–Eternal, co–Substantial, and One, but it is necessary to study and finally to attain direct vision of each one of the three propositions that have to be studied independently, as we have seen in the 'doctrine of the three omnisciences' that form Divine Omniscience—if we are going to clarify in our Mind the Divine Elements, we have to combine (the two) in order to produce the third element, and finally to see in direct vision the three Divine Elements combined in a union of Eternal inseparability.

Thus the profound Innate Awareness of the Ultimate possible Realization of True Enlightenment is the direct Innate Awareness of the Unity of God and this is the Highest Form possible, and consequently the one with the utmost power of transformation, because it is possible to approach it only in The State of a triple vision of the three Divine Elements that compose the Divine Ultimate Supreme Reality. When this super State of Pure Transcendental Knowledge of the Oneness of God is attained, it comes like a flash, known to the Greek Tradition as the "thunderbolt of the Divine Architect" or Demiurge who creates by way of the Divine Forms. Curiously enough, the image of the thunderbolt, as the appearance in the Mind of

True Enlightenment, is a well–known figure of Mahayana Buddhism, where the Adamantine Mind appears in the *Uttara Tantra* as the "immaculate, all–pervading Wisdom, imperishable, firm, quiescent, Eternal, and motionless."

Because Divine Wisdom has Divine Omniscience as its precedent, it receives the three fundamental Divine Omnisciences, each one corresponding to one of the Super Forms of the Trinity. As we have seen, the Form of the triple Divine Omnisciences means the complete illumination in our Mind in three separate Forms. We have to observe carefully that we say Divine Omniscience is produced in an illuminative, contemplative State where we come to intuit or to have the direct intuition of each one of the Super Divine Forms, but they are illuminative only in the sense that they illuminate each one of the Divine Elements by way of that special Knowledge, that Gnosis to which I referred at the beginning of this book. This Knowledge is one that does not refer to particulars, but only to the Universal and consequently, the Transcendental, beyond ordinary experience. The characteristic of this Knowledge, in a State of Divine Omniscience, means that by a powerful insight it produces a global understanding and a special Knowledge of 'wholes.' When this global understanding of each one of the Divine Elements is produced, we have three illuminations or three omnisciences, meaning global or Total Universal Knowledge.

But though these illuminations in the deepest State of meditation—composed of the quiescence of the ground of the Mind and its clarity, an openness like boundless space—produce omniscience, it is not yet Absolute Enlightenment, which means the vision by means of contemplative meditation of the three omniscient illuminations becoming one—a perfectly unified experience of the three as one, and yet independent without being separate. This is the State of real, True Enlightenment, the State that corresponds to the Form of Divine Wisdom. The Form of Divine Wisdom, as the true understanding of the Oneness of the Absolute Divine God or the Absolute Mind of Total Transcendence beyond concepts, mind structures, and language, is a Universal Super Form that produces that very special Divine Knowledge or Divine Gnosis that totally and radically transforms the point of view from one that is individual, narrow and self-centered to one that is beyond the limitations of the ego; and because it is not self-centered, it has the quality of openness as Space and also the quality of Pure Innate Awareness which has as its object the contemplation of Pure Innate Awareness or Pure Light with no conceptualization whatsoever. This State of Emptiness of the ground is not nothing, because it is full of the Pure Light that is also empty of concepts or language.

Thus, Divine Wisdom starts by realizing the three illuminative omnisciences before producing the synthesis for the actual State of Enlightenment. This State, at the beginning of Divine Wisdom, appears as a flash of Sudden Enlightenment, where the experience of Infinite Space with perfect Innate Awareness of it becomes a realized factual and actually experienced complete Truth. This actual complete Truth of an enlightened individual or a Sage is such because they live in the Enlightened State of Pure Innate Awareness, while living a relative, ordinary life. This is the True Gnosis, the synthetic union of the three

Divine Elements and the entering into the Divine Knowledge of the perfect Oneness of God. This is Divine Gnosis of True Enlightenment; this is Divine Wisdom.

The Form of Divine Wisdom or Divine Gnosis was the foundational Form of the Archaic Wisdom, the *philosophia perennis* that comes from the beginning of human culture. This specific knowledge is the theme of the oldest epic of humanity, the Sumerian *Epic of Gilgamesh*. The hero faces the question of death and to find the answer, he starts his quest for immortality, a quest for that which is unchanged, stable and Eternal. He journeys to the other side of the ocean to the Islands of Bliss, home to an immortal being, the only survivor of the Flood (the Sumerian Noah), and the only one who knows about immortality. Once Gilgamesh finds this Sage, he is instructed to go into the depths of the ocean where he will find a sacred plant, and he is told to bring back the plant that gives immortality. After he accomplishes this feat and returns with the plant, he is so tired from the journey that he rests at the side of the pool of pure water where he washes himself, and leaves the plant unattended. Meanwhile, a serpent who lives in the reeds by the pool steals the plant of immortality from Gilgamesh.

The extraordinary clarity of the symbols of this epic have been the theme of scholars of ancient archaic cultures. The ocean represents life in ordinary experience or the empirical experience of the world. The islands beyond the empirical world are the Islands of Bliss and Immortality where the Sage lives and they represent that State beyond the empirical state which is full of bliss and immortality. Yet Gilgamesh has to conquer his own Soul by going into the depths of his Innermost

Self, now not only beyond the empirical world but also at the depth of what sustains that empirical world—in fact, into the depth of his Innermost Self, where he finds the sacred plant of immortality that is his Higher Self. Coming back from his journey into the depths, he loses his attention to the sacred plant and because of this, the serpent of the ordinary world robs Gilgamesh of his precious Knowledge.

But it is in the *Gathas* of the Persian Prophet Spitama Zarathustra where the theology of the Light of Consciousness is perfectly defined, including the seven Divine Forces or Divine Attributes of the only One God, Ahura Mazda. In the sixth century BC, Cyrus the Great, who conquered Mesopotamia and Babylon, introduced there the religion of Zarathustra. Soon after, Pythagoras, who was studying in Egypt, was taken as a prisoner to Babylon with other high Egyptian priests. We know from his biography that he studied in Babylon with the Persian Magi for some twelve years. This fact gives the right indications about the origin of the Pythagorean theories of the Sacred Numbers which remind us of the Persian Divine Forces, seven in number. Pythagoras also has only seven numbers because the one, the Unity, and the two, the Dyad, were not considered numbers but the actual seed of them. But it is necessary to see that it was Socrates in whom we find for the first time the 'doctrine of the Light' in its sacred emanations, and the doctrine that there is another Consciousness besides our conscious Self that is transcendent and has the characteristics of simplicity, homogeneity and clarity of Pure Innate Awareness. This 'Consciousness in itself' is immovable, yet full of understanding, not by intellectual discrimination, but by intuitive Perfect Forms.

Scholars in Classical Greek philosophy have treated the Socratic question "What is Man?" as an incisive question, trying to prove that his interlocutors did not know anything and in this way, annoying them and making lots of enemies in the process. But it is with Werner Jaeger in his well–known book, *Paideia,* that modern scholarship shows with clear insight that the Socratic question is not just a haranguing of an agent provocateur, but that Socrates brings for the first time to Greek philosophy the answer to the Socratic question, namely, "Man is his Soul." As Jaeger points out, there is an unavoidable religious factor in this answer, and Socrates is described by his friends as always speaking about the Soul with religious fervor. As Aristotle observed and as is repeated in the famous phrase of Cicero, "Socrates brought philosophy down from heaven to earth." More accurately, we can say "from heaven to man" since the central question was no longer about natural science or what is the Ultimate Matter of the *physiologoi* or the Orphic–Pythagorean theology of a Soul independent from the body.

However, it was Socrates who answered for the first time the question "What is Man?" with "Man is his Soul." By Soul, Socrates meant a conscious Self. Thus, we have the formula "Know thyself," which was the archaic motto of the Oracle at Delphi. The most powerful Socratic formula is that we do not live the life of our own Soul because we do not know anything about it. The most important point is that only in that Consciousness, which is Self–aware, can human beings find happiness, fulfillment, peace, and the bliss of living in the State of Innate Awareness of the Soul, which has to be carefully purified from its own hindrances, attachments and fetters of the material and the social world. Thus, the Socratic revolution means a complete turnaround of values, where the values of the material world—wealth, power, pleasures—lose complete importance in front of the spiritual values of the Soul which is naturally directed toward the Divine Light of the One Good God. This image of the Soul, as a servant of God, with no other value or interest than this one, is the foundational rock of all Greek, Hellenistic and Roman doctrines of Enlightenment and Mystical Transcendence by way of a virtuous life. The Socratic virtue is only one, as he proves in the first of Plato's *Dialogues*, known as the "Socratic Dialogues." In each one of these Dialogues, Socrates inquires about courage, temperance, fidelity, and so on, and after a skillful cross–examination, he proves his interlocutor incapable of defining the proposed virtue. But what is paradoxical in these Dialogues is that they finish abruptly, as if everyone got tired with their discussion and went on with their own business. Thus, these Dialogues are an open question that scholars before Jaeger interpreted as the famous Socratic irony, somehow unpleasant and rather impertinent.

After Jaeger's *Paideia*, modern scholars agreed that Socrates was analyzing the one virtue from different angles, but the sum of them gives us, as a result, the understanding that virtue is an internal Self–ness or a basic energy by which a consciousness in Perfect Innate Awareness is also the internal Perfect Witness. This is to say, the Soul is transcendental and spiritual. Socrates gave this one virtue the name of "excellence" or the authentic *arete* (Gk), and this excellent energy was basically ethical and in that sense manifested under different aspects, but the excellence of the purity of Consciousness as its maximum Good is again the foundation of all the practice by first purifying consciousness and then by cultivating this transcendental virtue that is the Soul, or an Innate Awareness which is Intelligent and Self–conscious. In sum, this is a Divine Knowledge, a Divine Gnosis or Divine Wisdom.

As a result of Divine Wisdom or the State of Enlightened Innate Awareness, Socrates posits the attainment of Super States that were crystallized in the sense that they acquired permanency and stability, which he called *enkrateia* (Gk) or self–control, *eleutheria* (Gk) or liberty, and *autarkeia* (Gk) or independence. Self–control here means not an act of willpower but control of the self in its meaning of awareness of what is Intelligent and Pure and the direct Knowledge of that Pure Intellect. Here is the basic method for sustaining the State of Pristine Completeness without thought constructs, by way of controlling the entire Self, Soul or Innate Awareness without losing the actual participation with the empirical world. If this is attained, this State of continuous self–control will maintain us in direct contact with the Absolute and Universal. By liberty (*eleutheria*), Socrates understood the freedom of the Logos, which is the consciousness that was at the very beginning of ourselves, being the most pure and directly Divine. By independence (*autarkeia*), Socrates meant the self–sufficiency of The Good and the State of Enlightened Self which, in its purity, can have that direct vision of the Light of Pure Intelligence or Divine Gnosis or Knowledge of the Unity of God.

Modern scholarship agrees that the ethical way toward self–enlightenment and realization became the cornerstone of all Greek philosophy after Socrates. But besides Classical Platonism and Aristotelianism, the Ethical schools are of enormous importance in understanding the doctrines and practices of enlightenment. We need to refer very briefly to the most important of them. Perhaps of all these schools, the one that was founded by Antisthenes, the Cynic School, is the most radical of all the Socratic schools, and in this sense, the founder of the true monastic life of wandering, celibate monks, who have renounced all the goods of the world, as well as all the traps of the mind by an inquiry into the names of objects only, without participating with any other relation. If we say the car is green, there is no relation between car and green. They are both different objects. This breaking–up or deconstruction of the relativity of the empirical world of the Cynics reminds us of Nagarjuna's breaking of relativity by way of codependent causation and eliminating the entire Relative Mind in its totality in both the Cynic and Madhyamika Traditions. The Cynics, these itinerant saints who had nothing in life, followed only the most immediate and most simple needs of life. As they liked to put it, they lived the life of a dog—hence, their name, Cynic (like a dog)—because of their unconventional life, not attached to anything. Most paradoxically, of course, they lived in a State of Bliss. These ascetics were found all around the Mediterranean at the time of Christianity's birth, and it is almost inevitable to trace a comparison between the Cynics and the first Christians, who embraced almost the same values. Of course, cynicism has a very dubious connotation in our time, but the "dogs" of antiquity lived only with the attention, that is, their total Innate Awareness directed to the Inner Master to be found in the center of the heart, which was expressed in their famous "Prayer of the Heart," and which was transferred into Christianity by the Desert Fathers. The Cynics did not theorize because they would deconstruct any theory, and so they were existential practitioners of Innate Awareness, Light and Gnosis, and the first true mystical ascetics of antiquity.

Aristippus, a close friend of Socrates, founded the Cyrenaic School in the city of Cyrene, where his wealthy family lived. He confirmed the Socratic 'doctrine of *autarkeia*' or the independence of the Wise Man, who would keep his pure Self–consciousness or a constant remembering of the Transcendental Self in such a way that he would always move correctly, even if he is surrounded by the splendor of a wealthy life, where pleasures are always considered good. The State of Innate Awareness was not obscured by a fatal attachment to those pleasures and he did not become actually forgetful of the State of constant Innate Awareness or the enlightened point of view that does not forget for a second that all phenomena are just appearances, not to be taken seriously, nor to compromise the purity of Enlightenment. This was considered a method of Self–awareness of the utmost sophistication, and it reminds us quite strongly of the doctrines of 'crazy wisdom' in Ch'an–Zen Buddhism and Dzogchen.

The Socratic 'doctrine of Enlightenment' is based on deconstructing the Relative Mind of concepts, language and inferred knowledge by way of observing that actual knowledge of the relative phenomenal empirical mind is untenable and basically absurd because of the relativity of all mental constructs. Thus, the famous Socratic dictum "I only know that I know nothing, and even that I do not know." Old scholarship points out that this was a proof either of the humbleness of Socrates or perhaps of the ironic mood of the old devil but, with modern scholarship, it is necessary to take Socrates seriously. Thus we have to interpret the Socratic dictum as a perfect description of a State of Mind of Non–conceptualization—empty of conceptual thinking and discrimination about those conceptions.

Pyrrho of Elis, the founder of the Skeptic School, took the Socratic doctrines of deconstruction of the Relative Mind of Concepts and Language to their most radical and extreme conclusion. Pyrrho established a method for presenting the relativity of the mind and its concepts with extreme logical accuracy: all concepts were relative, and we could not impute to them solid and conclusive Truth. This methodic deconstruction was systematized by Aenesidemus. The point here is that Pyrrho postulated doctrines which, in front of the absurdity of the Relative Mind, if we were honest and authentic, would produce a suspension of judgment (*epoche*) or, in other words, a suspension of the mind's function of thinking and comparing, and by this means, entering into the State of *Ataraxia* or a Mind of Transcendence of the world of appearances, and entering into a State of complete lucidity—a Mind in a State of Perfect Silence and Pure Light. We have to remember that Pyrrho was considered a totally realized, enlightened Sage, and a Saint, who had purified his Soul to the Perfect State of direct Union with the Divine.

Pyrrho's deconstruction system reminds us strikingly of the methods of mind reduction such as *Vipashyana* (Skt), which consists of deconstructing relative thoughts by observing them from the point of view of the Absolute Mind which is the origin and source of the relative thoughts that arise and dissolve in the Absolute Mind of Non–conceptualization. *Samatha* (Skt) or the 'Mind in itself' that is quiescent and clear is the twin method which in Pyrrho is the *epoche* (Skt) or reduction of thought and the *ataraxia* or quiescence of Mind. The combination of *Samatha* and *Vipashyana* (Skt) is the most fundamental method in all transcendental meditation, most especially in the doctrines of Ch'an–Zen, Mahamudra, Dzogchen, and Atiyoga. But it is in the Neoplatonic schools of Alexandria where the 'doctrine of a Mind of Enlightenment,' with the doctrines of spiritual and mystical asceses by way of meditation and contemplation, acquires its full maturity. The sophistication of the Platonic mystics can be observed in the following synthesis of Numenius, a Middle Platonic, of great importance to Neoplatonism.

THE ROAD TO UNDERSTANDING OF THE GOOD

Bodies have to be perceived by tokens which reside in contiguous objects. But not from any cognizable object can The Good be deduced. Only by an illustration can we explain how to attain an understanding of The Good. It is as if one were sitting on an observation tower and watching intently and should at a glance discover a little solitary fishing

> boat, sailing along between the waves. Thus, far from the visible world, he must commune with The Good, being alone with the alone (solitude), far from man, or a living being, or anybody small or great, in an inexpressible, indefinable, immediately Divine solitude. There, in the radiant beauty, dwells The Good, brooding over existence in a manner which though solitary and dominating, is both peaceful, gracious and friendly.
>
> To imagine that one sees The Good floating up to oneself is entirely wrong; and to suppose that he has approached The Good is nothing less than impudent, so long as he dallies with the sense–world. For the approach to The Good is not easy, but what you might call divinely difficult. The best way is to neglect the whole visible world, courageously to attack the sciences, and to contemplate numbers; thus is attained meditation on what is The One.

In the most lucid way, Numenius gives us a complete and synthetic course in meditation to attain Transcendence and Oneness with God. Here are all the main elements of transcendental contemplation. We also find profound examples of contemplative transcendence in the *Hermetica,* Book 1, the *Poimandres*. We read in the sixth point:

> "That light is I, even Mind, the first God, who was before the watery substance which appeared out of the darkness; and the Word which came forth from the Light is the son of God." "How so?" said I. "Learn

> my meaning," said he, "by looking at what you yourself have in you; for in you too, the word is son, and the mind is father of the word. They are not separate one from the other; for life is the union of word and mind." Thus has spoken Poimandres.

In the great Neoplatonic system of Plotinus, there exist three Fundamental Principles of a One Transcendental Good God, the Divine Creator; the Demiurge, who represents the spiritual world—whose content is the Divine Forms or the archetypal Universal concepts that must be understood as the thought of God; and finally, the Cosmos, which Plato described as "the living, existing Soul." Plotinus calls these three Divine and Ultimate Principles "the One God, the Intellectual Principle, and the Soul." The 'Intellectual Principle in itself' has as its content the Intellectual Principle proper, the *Nous,* and the Divine Forms (Ideas), the *Noeta* (Gk); and the synthesis of both, the *Noesis* (Gk).

This Neoplatonic doctrine reappears in Kant as a 'doctrine of foundationalism' which posits an Ultimate Ground that he calls the "noumenal substrate of myself," or the Mind as it is which we can only grasp by way of a "transcendental apperception," and the world of representation or the world of phenomena that is grasped by "empirical apperception." Schopenhauer declared himself the real inheritor of Kant's 'doctrine of the noumenal and phenomenal worlds,' which he expounded upon in his classical *The World as Will and Idea.* Husserl's phenomenological reduction proposes to find the Pure Idea or Kant's *noumena* or, as he calls it, the Platonic "*eideia*" that can be isolated and purified by "bracketing" the entire phenomenal reality with a suspension of judgment or the *epoche* of Pyrrho the Skeptic.

Integral Philosophy posits the 'doctrine of Divine Wisdom' as an outcome of Divine Omniscience, which provides the integral three Divine Elements. The first omniscience is represented by the Natural Mind or by apprehending the nature of the Mind, which is found to be quiescent, simple and Eternal; the second omniscience is that the actual content of this Divine Primordial Mind is the spiritual world of the nine Divine Forms; and finally, the third omniscience is to conceive the Relative Mind under the global and totalizing view, the view of Divine Omniscience that finds that all reality is nothing but a projection of the mind, and thus all relative terms are not different but composed from the same substance, this is to say, of thought itself. Once the three omnisciences are clearly presented, it is possible to unify the three of them in such a way that they are grasped together as one substance, and this new Knowledge is the Knowledge of Enlightenment or Divine Gnosis, which essentially means the Unity of the three Divine Elements in the 'One and Only.' This most fundamental truth is presented in the Arica Declaration of the Unity of God where:

GOD IS ETERNAL—Absolute Principle

IS IN ALL OF US—Intellectual Principle

IS IN EVERYTHING—Spiritual Synthetic Principle

IS ONE WITHOUT SECOND—Unitary Principle of True Enlightenment or Divine Gnosis

Thus Divine Wisdom, in Protoanalysis, also means Divine

Work since the process of attaining Divine Wisdom or Gnosis is the actual work that produces the clarification and divinization of our Natural Soul.

MENTATIONAL ANALYSIS OF DIVINE WISDOM

1 **SUBSTANCE** (What is it?) Divine Wisdom is the perception of the Absolute Present that opens the Pure Light of Gnosis.

2 **FORM** (How is it?) The Pure Light of Gnosis appears as a transparency of Innate Awareness.

3 **POSSIBILITIES** (Why originated?) Divine Wisdom has as its immediate origin Divine Omniscience, or the view of reality as a whole or 'Mind–only.'

4 **NEEDS** (What purpose?) Divine Wisdom liberates the mind from matter, as well as from subjectivity.

5 **IMPULSE** (What intention?) Divine Wisdom discloses the Spirit or the Mind in what are otherwise material and unstable phenomena.

6 **METHOD** (How accomplished?) Divine Wisdom is accomplished by continuously sustaining the liberation of the Mind.

7 **STANDARD** (What is the ideal?) The continuous presence of the Super Form of Divine Gnosis (Knowledge) is the realization of Divine Wisdom.

8 **ORIENTATION** (What is the direction?) Divine Wisdom, because it is only disclosed in Pure Present, has no horizontal direction of time, but only a vertical direction of space which points to the perfect center where there is no movement and from where all movement originates.

9 **CAPACITY** (What is the strength?) Divine Wisdom means a Mind of Liberation and Enlightenment.

10 **CHARISMA** (What is the appearance?) When we become aware of the subtle Pure Light of the Mind and we have actual vision of the Light, Divine Wisdom appears as a subtle violet mist which produces an actual infusion of Light that appears to illuminate the objects of our external environment.

11 **MEANS** (How produced?) By continuous liberation of the Mind, we disclose the Form and experience of Divine Wisdom.

12 **GOALS** (What is attained?) Divine Wisdom is the crystallization of Divine Gnosis as Total Perfection or the point of view of the Pure Light of Gnosis.

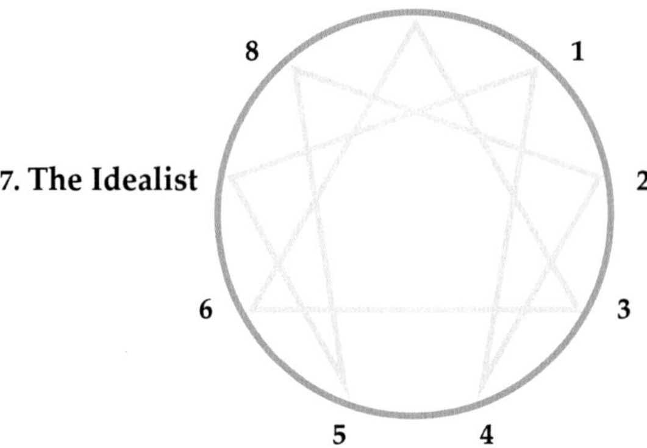

THE FIXATION OF THE IDEALIST

In the Enneagram of the Fixations of the Existential Mind (Sphere 15), the fixated point 7 is the Idealist. Like all the terms that characterize the Ego–Fixations in Protoanalysis, the Idealist is described with some sense of mockery by pointing to the fact that by virtue of the Defense Mechanism, the Ego–Fixation is constantly over–exaggerating itself. In this way, the Idealist (point 7) is not generally conceived as a romantic visionary but rather a person who is plagued with ideas and plans of all sorts, because the Form of Divine Wisdom is lost and replaced by the Ego–Fixation of the Idealist. Then there comes the obscuration of the Divine Form and with it the Innate Awareness of the Divine Plan that can only be perceived in the Being of Pure Presence, which makes possible real work in the sense of disclosing the State of Innate Awareness and the Wisdom of Pure Gnosis and their omniscient perception of Total Reality. Instead, it is replaced by the Ego–Fixation, where the direction is reversed and is no longer going with the Divine Flow, following the Divine Plan and thus producing a real Spiritual Work that can only be done on the grounds of Pure Presence and Reality. The Idealists, with their narrow and fixated point of view, will find themselves to be without any orientation, in the sense of being lost without knowing where or how to go. Because of this sense of being lost, the ego of the Idealist will structure their point of view by surrounding themselves with a constant plan for the future and an acute criticism of the past. Things were never done as they should have been, and new and better plans should be proposed, discussed and followed. This, of course, never becomes a reality, because the planning itself of the Idealist is based on the unreal point of view of an ego that lives in the past and projects itself into the future. But neither the past nor the future are, in fact, real or present, and thus the Idealist does not live as a real Being, but as an inauthentic being who lives in what was in the past and is not any longer, and of what is in the future and is not yet, and thus it is not. This is what Heidegger would term an "inauthentic being" who lives in a condition of dreaming about the past and imagining the future, bypassing the real being of the present.

Thus, Divine Wisdom appears only in the Pure Present, transcends time, and has a grasp of Eternity, because Divine Wisdom reflects in itself that there is no beginning or end, that with complete certitude it is immortal. When this insight has been discovered through Divine Wisdom, our perception of the past—as being the cause of the present, or understanding the influence of past action as karma, or that the toll of the lower aspects of our past actually produces the present situation—dissolves and disappears. This view of Eternity that comes from Divine Wisdom has the extreme power of liberating all the subjective and material perceptions of reality. Thus, Divine Wisdom has the unique power of liberating the mind from all attachments manifesting as subjective emotions and bad memories which are framed in suffering, with a sense of being disoriented and totally lost, which is the main characteristic of point 7, the Idealist. By this power of liberation and Enlightenment, Divine Wisdom dissolves all appearances, external as well as internal, into what they really are—the manifestation of Divine Wisdom or Divine Gnosis.

This is the real meaning of the contemplation of the Forms throughout the Cosmos, in the Platonic sense of abstracting the spiritual element in whatever we perceive and acknowledge, not only as a matter perceived, but as a mental form given to that matter. For instance, while seeing a chair, the matter is the wood of which it is fabricated and the form is the chair and, of course, it is a complete mental proposition. The form is in the chair and is inseparable from its material elements, as Aristotle observed in his 'hylomorphic doctrine of reality' or the inseparability of matter and form. But the point is that the forms are, strictly speaking, of a mental nature, as Plato indicates, since obviously a chair, without someone perceiving that bundle of matter as a chair, has no sense and, as a chair, it would be non–existent. When we perceive this point of view of Divine Wisdom that dissolves all matter into Spirit in the sense that all our perceptions are, in fact, just mental operations, and when we understand its nature, the 'appearance in itself' becomes automatically, instantaneously liberated. This liberation is the radical triumph over the subjective and asleep dream–like point of view of the ego of the Idealist and their endless planning of the future and criticism of the past.

EGO–REDUCTION OF THE IDEALIST

Because the Idealist distorts reality by their projection of being inferiorized by their siblings or the world which provokes tension in them, they react to this internal process with the Existential Attitudes of Fear and Stress, which give them the outward appearance of being a "nervous wreck." The ego–delusion of the Idealist is to imagine themselves as Great Planners. Their Passion is Gluttony in the sense of grasping everything beyond their ability and capacity. The Dichotomy of the Idealist is Superiority on one side and Inferiority on the other. Their Primary Defense Mechanism is Displacement by which they redirect desires or impulses from the original object to a more acceptable substitute. For example, they may "take out" their anger at their boss by shouting at a family member. The Idealist's ego–position is their Self–importance. They use the ego–balancer of "I have confidence and self–respect" in order to face reality. The Idealist's ego–difficulty is that of a Dreamer. Their ego–reaction is one of Capriciousness due to their own plans. The ego–justification of the Idealist uses Hypocrisy and Double–talk. The Door of Compensation that they use is Debauchery of all material pleasures, which helps to calm their nervousness. Their Dichotomic Existential Attitudes are to be Impartial on one side and Inferiorizing on the other. Their way is to find Presence in themselves and that will take them to their Trap of Idealism. Idealism is conducive to opening the Form of Divine Wisdom through which they liberate themselves from their Fixation.

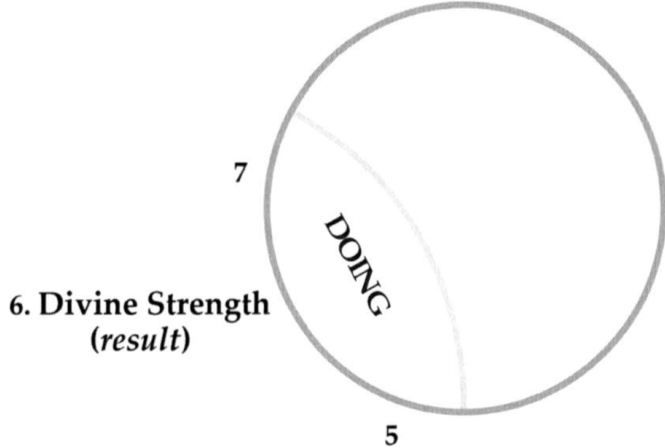

DIVINE STRENGTH (Point 6)

Divine Strength is the *resulting* (sustaining) point in the triad of the Doing Group, which is suspended from the Super Form of Divine Gnosis or Universal Spirit. Thus, Divine Strength as point 6 of the enneagram is one of the points of the internal triangle of the enneagram that point to the Super Forms of Being and God (point 9); the Good Man (point 3); and Gnosis or the Universal Spirit (point 6). This super triad is the foundation or the *function* of the enneagram where each one of the points in themselves becomes a triad produced by their internal movement. As we have seen, the schema is applicable to the three Instincts, which are the functions of the Enneagram of the Fixations. The Form of Divine Strength is one of total certitude that our True Self equates with Self–knowledge, which is nothing but the view into the nature of our Mind. When we find that Natural Mind, which is beyond conceptualization and which is 'Intellect in itself,' we have found a Mind to which we are in immediate and approximate contact, and with which we have an intuitive, direct relationship without the duality of thinking in terms of concepts and language.

Aristotle called this the "Superior Mind," the first *entelechy* (Gk) that is just pure thought; its content is the reasoning process of discrimination and judgment, the second entelechy. Plotinus assigned the term of *Nous,* commonly translated as Mind, to the first entelechy or Pure Intellect, and *Noeta* for the second entelechy or the mind of phenomena. It also applies to Kant's distinction between noumena or the 'thing in itself' and the phenomena or the appearances of the mind. When we disclose the nature of our Mind, we have at the same time found our True Self, one that is Universal, infinitely open, peaceful, and totally assured by the certitude of a complete action. This axiomatic certitude is what is disclosed by the Form of Divine Strength. Thus, when entering into the conception of Divine

Strength, we are affirming the certitude that our True Self is not only Pure Mind but Pure Mind of Gnosis or the Light of Understanding in which Logos can be further described as Divine Spirit and the Logos, the Divine Spirit in man; in the same way that Divine Good is the Divine Logos in man; and the Divine Being is God in man. These three aspects of the great super triad that sustains the Enneagram of the Divine Forms are presented in the Arica Declaration of the Unity of God.

Thus, the Form of Divine Strength is to have an Objective Faith, which means that it is not based upon our subjective ego–centered point of view, but in our Essential Nature itself, in the certitude of the Universal Entelechy or the infinite *Nous*. This means certitude in the Divine part of our being since Aristotle insisted that the first entelechy or the 'Intellect as such' was the only immortal part of the Soul and the only one that survives and transcends death. To have certitude about our own True Self, once we recognize its nature, is to have the absolute sense of certitude that is produced in us by the undeniability of the nature of the Mind that is equated with the True Self or our Higher Self which is immortal, blissful and Pure Gnosis (Knowledge). Once we discover that the nature of our Mind is this Pure and unbounded Light of Innate Awareness, we become truly enlightened, because the Pure Light of Divine Wisdom shines upon the Divine Strength of our immortal, perfect and complete Higher Self.

Thus this direct experience of the Essential Nature of ourselves has been realized in a Pure State of a Mind of Non–conceptualization and non–duality, the Enlightened Mind (Sphere 9), where the Light of the Unity of the two Minds (Absolute and Relative) provides the realization of the Ornamental Mind, whose point of view is that all is actually just Pure Mind, first entelechy or the *Nous*. This is so because the Relative Mind, the second entelechy or *Noeta,* is nothing but the movement of appearances in the mind. Plato applied his famous allegory of the cavern where the *Nous* is the Pure Light of the Sun, and the *Noeta* are the shadows that could be seen against the walls of the cavern, where the shadows are actually only partial projections produced by the fire in the cavern and are completely dependent upon it. There is also the great metaphor of Heraclitus, who insisted that the mind was like a river in whose waters you could never step twice. This clearly indicates the constant flow of the water of the river. Unfortunately, since Aristotle, the doctrine of Heraclitus has been interpreted as one that reality itself is nothing but a permanent flow and, quite superficially, he came to be known as the philosopher of "the flow," and what was forgotten was that Heraclitus was clearly showing that the uninterrupted, ever–changing flow of the waters of the river was only possible due to the existence of the 'river in itself' or the river bed over which the water flowed. This metaphor points out the permanency and unchangeable nature of the river, regardless of the impermanence or transitory nature of its water. Here the riverbed represents the Absolute Mind, the first entelechy or *Nous,* and the water represents the Relative Mind, the second entelechy or *Noeta.*

Thus, we enter into the State of Divine Strength by the Innate Awareness or the direct insight into the True Nature of the Mind, which is found to be Universal, transparent, perfect, and the complete Pure Light of Gnosis. Once we have experienced Divine Strength, this gives us the supreme conviction that can be characterized as Objective Faith in the reality that the True Self is Divine as well as Immortal. When we attain this State of Divine Strength, a profound Security with a Calm–abiding Peace crystallizes in our Immortal Soul as a Pure Spiritual State, and it will never abandon us once it has been genuinely experienced, not as a concept or definition but as a profound reality of the Divine Nature of our Higher Self. Because this nature is found to be Divine, it is akin to the Universal Spirit, and also to the Logos or The Good and the One Being or God. This contemplation of the Divine Strength is the Knowledge of the nature of our True Self which gives us an immense transformative power because it can change the direction of our life from the relative and ego–fixated point of view to an objective and Universal point of view that produces the constant Knowledge of the Divine Nature of our True Self. This transformative power of Objective Faith is simply unbreakable, because it has a certitude that goes beyond all doubt.

This is not a certitude beyond doubt in the sense of Descartes' *cogito ergo sum* (Lat) or "I think, therefore I am," because the Cartesian "cogito" is based on the existence of doubt and in the impossibility of denying the existence of 'doubt in itself,' for to do so is logically contradictory. Thus, doubt is the principle of all reasoning, judging or thinking. Doubt is duality and, as such, the principle. Therefore, what Descartes is saying to us is that because he has doubts, he is thinking, and because he is thinking, "cogito," he can affirm his own existence and being. The "cogito" is a product of doubtful thinking and belongs to the Relative Mind, which blocks or destroys the absolute pure entelechy or *Nous*, which is beyond the thinking and the doubt of the "cogito." Thus, as Husserl points out, real Being appears only when the thinking process of the "cogito" has been bracketed or suspended, producing the State of *Epoche* of the ancient skepticism of Pyrrho. This State of *Epoche* where we find the Natural Mind as it is before the appearance of a thinking process due to the doubts of the relative "cogito," is of infinite transformative power, for Divine Strength is the one Divine Form that gives us the Innate Awareness of the Divine Gnosis, which is the Knowledge of the Essential Nature of the Mind.

MENTATIONAL ANALYSIS OF DIVINE STRENGTH

1 **SUBSTANCE** (What is it?) Divine Strength is the Objective Faith that the Essential Nature of the Self is Transcendental and Divine Pure Gnosis.

2 **FORM** (How is it?) Divine Strength appears as an unbreakable and constant Objective Faith in the True Self.

3 **POSSIBILITIES** (Why originated?) Divine Strength has its origin in Divine Wisdom or the Transcendental Gnosis.

4 **NEEDS** (What purpose?) Divine Strength is the supreme Refuge and support in the journey of the Spirit.

5 **IMPULSE** (What intention?) Divine Strength is the main transformational Form that gives the Soul a new transcendental outlook that entirely changes the concept of life and death.

6 **METHOD** (How accomplished?) Divine Strength is attained by the direct view into the Essential Nature of the Mind.

7 **STANDARD** (What is the ideal?) The final ideal of Divine Strength is the total certitude in the Divinity of the Self.

8 **ORIENTATION** (What is the direction?) Divine Strength has as its direction the complete and perfect Self–realization of the Mind.

9 **CAPACITY** (What is the strength?) Divine Strength is the conviction in the permanency and immortality of the True Self.

10 **CHARISMA** (What is the appearance?) Divine Strength gives us a sense of profound security, peace and the deep Innate Awareness of Divine Presence in the vision of the subtle emerald–green Light of the Mind.

11 **MEANS** (How produced?) Divine Strength is disclosed by a direct vision into the True Nature of the Mind.

12 **GOALS** (What is attained?) Divine Strength produces the permanency of the objective Awakened State and the appearance of the Ornamental Mind.

THE FIXATION OF THE ADVENTURER

In the Enneagram of the Fixations of the Existential Mind (Sphere 15), the fixated point 6 is the Adventurer which, in its Protoanalytical characterization, is not that of the heroic adventurer who puts themselves into discoveries of all sorts or in great journeys full of new experiences and whose reward is the finding of new knowledge, but is that of a person who

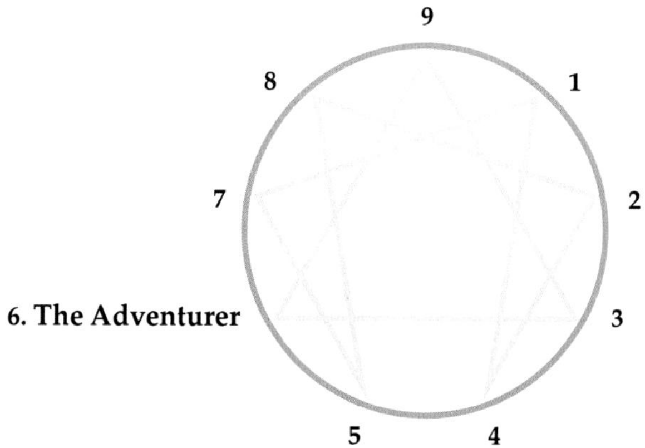

is fixated in point 6 because of the loss of the Form of Divine Strength or Objective Faith. Consequently, the Adventurer's main characteristic is a total lack of faith in themselves, in other human beings, and in God. Thus, the Adventurer thinks they are completely lost and alone in the world, since for them it is hard to believe in the Goodness of 'Humanity as such,' and also in their own Goodness. Because of this, the Adventurer is profoundly distrustful of God, humankind and even the world, and in a very deep sense, distrustful of the Goodness of their own ability. Thus the subjective Polar Preconception that protects the ego against the degenerate, deceitful world appears with full strength in the Adventurer; and with this constant superstition and neurotic paranoia of being persecuted, misled, lied to, and even more, because of their lack of faith in themselves, the Adventurer strongly manifests the Existential Attitudes of Fear and Stress, which permeate the triad of the Doing Group. Because the Adventurer is the *resulting* (sustaining) mode of the triad, the subjective Existential Attitudes of Fear and Stress are especially acute. Because of this constant distrust, suspicion and fear, every single event or situation becomes an adventure of major proportions, like killing mosquitoes with a shotgun. Because of this constant fearful state, the basic ego–delusion of the Adventurer is that they are engaging in dangerous and fearful situations in which they are being used and exploited. Thus, they develop a cynical point of view that everybody is actually moved only by self–interest and self–gratification. Their lack of faith causes them to be internally very weak without any faith in themselves, making them extremely inconsequential, inconsistent and capable of changing positions and points of view without warning and applying their specific cynicism to their lack of consistency and consequence. This state of affairs, in which the Adventurer lives in fear and stress, makes them have the basic ego–delusion and a point of view in which, because they have no faith in themselves, they have a cowardly attitude, and they behave constantly as a "nervous wreck," whose ongoing fear and stress become manifested by their suspiciousness and by their hostile outbursts and constant shortcomings, always being insecure and not knowing if they are choosing the best and the right path or situation. Divine Strength is the antidote and the cure for the fearful, suspicious and cowardly Adventurer, point 6, whose cynicism is insufficient for covering the actual lack of faith in themselves that the innermost Being, our True Nature is, in fact, Divine, Immortal and belongs equally to all human beings.

EGO–REDUCTION OF THE ADVENTURER

The projection that fixates the Adventurer is that of believing they are useless in relation to their siblings or the world, which provokes tension in them and which develops the Existential Attitudes of Fear and Stress, making them outwardly manifest the character and behavior of a "nervous wreck." Their ego–delusion is one of Cowardice because they see everything across their exaggerated fear. The Passion of the Adventurer is Fear; they passionately promote an internal state of fear by being distrustful and by believing that they are constantly in imminent danger. The Dichotomy is Striving and Pushing on one side, and being Lazy and Indifferent on the other. Adventurers use the Primary Defense Mechanism of Projection by which unacceptable thinking, fears or behavior are rejected in themselves and projected onto another person, group, race, or religion. This Projection is without insight and acknowledgment of their own internal process. Their ego–position is one of a Self–defeating attitude. They use the ego–balancer of "I am responsible and relaxed," in order to deal with life. The Adventurer's difficulty is to be constantly frightened. Their ego–reaction is to become a libertine and an outgoing type of person to combat and hide their fear. They use the ego–justification of Calculation to accomodate their arguments for their own benefit. The Adventurer uses the Door of Compensation of Panic in order to escape from situations that they cannot control. Their Dichotomic Existential Attitude is Agreeable on one side and Overpowering on the other. The Adventurer finds their way out by Accomplishment, which opens the Trap of Security that will allow them to enter the Form of Divine Strength, which will dissolve their Fixation and its related process.

CHAPTER 5

THE PROCESS OF ACTUAL ENLIGHTENMENT

The process of Enlightenment by way of the Divine Forms starts, as we have seen, with a *katharsis* or a purification of each Fixation by using the Enneagram of the Fixations of the ego–personalities, which are clarified by ego–reduction with its concomitant fourteen steps or items ordered in fourteen enneagrams of process. The Method applied during this process corresponds to the first Law of Trialectics which defines a process as the nine steps that are necessary for producing a complete cycle. Proceeding in this way, it is possible to open the entire process as a 'unity in itself' and, consequently, to effectively dissolve the correlative Fixation which, in fact, is nothing but the obscuration of the Divine Form.

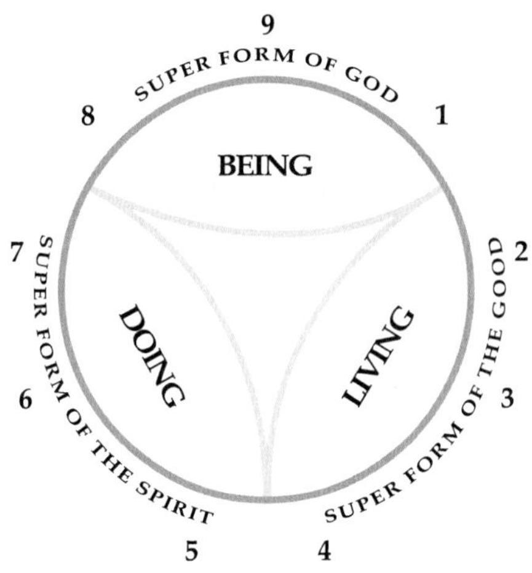

TRIAD OF THE SUPER FORMS

As we have seen, uniting the three Divine Omnisciences—or the Super Forms of the Divine Trinity of God, the Good Man, and Spiritual Consciousness—produces a clear result of contemplating the three Forms as one by the synthesis of the perennial philosophy in its law of the 'two becoming three.'

The same synthesis has to be produced at the level of the Divine Forms in accordance with the particular and individual Trifix by taking one Form of the corresponding groups of Being, Living and Doing. In the same way that Enlightenment actually means the contemplation of the three Divine Super Forms as being one and the same, Enlightenment at the level of the Divine Forms means the contemplation of the individual triad of Divine Forms corresponding to the Trifix, where the Form (Idea) of Being produces the Form (Idea) of Living and results in the Form (Idea) of Doing. When we see this internal circulation of the Divine Forms in ourselves by experiencing the three of them as being one and the same, we enter into a State of True Enlightenment.

THE DIVINE FORMS AND THE COGNITIVE MIND

As we have seen, the Divine Forms dissolve the Fixations at their very root in their instinctual imbalance. When the Fixations are dissolved by the actualization of the Divine Forms, the basic Instincts become cleansed and purified in such a way that they can perform their fundamental functions without the distortion produced by the Fixation with its fourteen attendant declensions or aspects which are found in a linear series. But, in accordance with Protoanalysis, the Instincts themselves provoke a lower level of Existential Attitudes because of the influence of the Polar Preconception, which can be defined as our basic attitude of distrust, fear and suspicion, and which is projected as aggressivity, passivity or indifference, which will influence the Instincts at their very root. In Integralism, the Primordial Mind (Sphere 16) is composed of the two Poles that frame the human psyche, known as the Sexual and Spiritual Poles. The five organic body Systems of the Somatic Mind (Sphere 18) project the functioning of the organs and glands as five elements which, in Protoanalysis, are understood as a determined state produced by the wavelength of the different energies manifested by the five organic Systems of the body. Thus, the five elements are the content of the Cognitive Mind (Sphere 17).

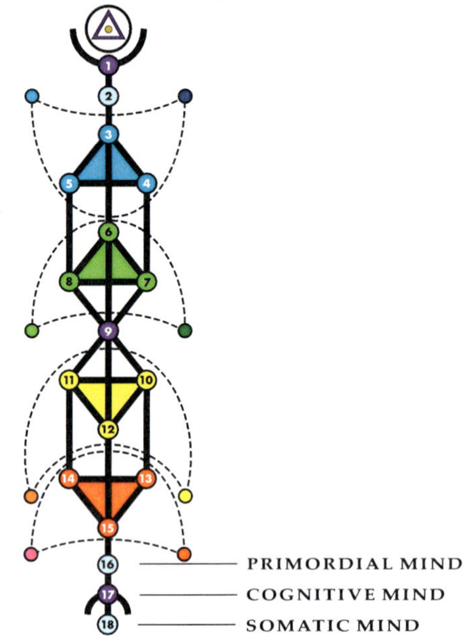

In Integral Philosophy, the five Elements are understood in the Platonic sense that the most basic forms are substance, motion, rest, same, and different. These most basic ideas have to be considered in the sense of forces, as were the four Elements of Empedocles known as water, air, earth, and fire. This series was completed with the Aristotelian "quintessence," later known as ether or consciousness. Integralism understands that the five Elements are divided in two sets in accordance with their essential functions. One set is the dynamic set composed of substance, motion and rest. These three elements are in constant interconnection because they depend on each other. In reality they can be defined as three forms of movement and, of course, movement cannot be understood without rest. Both movement and rest cannot be understood without a substance which moves and which can also be at rest.

EMPEDOCLES	PLATO	INTEGRALISM AND TRIALECTICS	POWERS OF VALENCES	NEOPLATONISM	ARISTOTLE AND HEGEL
WATER	SUBSTANCE	RESULT	(=)	SUSTAINING	SYNTHESIS
AIR	MOTION	ACTION	(+)	PROCEEDING	THESIS
EARTH	REST	REACTION	(–)	RETURNING	ANTITHESIS
ETHER	SAME	FUNCTION OF UNITY	(1)	ONE	SAME
FIRE	DIFFERENT	FUNCTION OF PLURALITY	(∞)	MANY	OTHER

CHART OF THE FIVE ELEMENTS

As the foundation of the Universe, these three Elements produce all the movement that Protoanalysis understands as dynamics and, as such, as powers. Thus, there is an *active* power (+), a *reactive* power (–), and a *resulting* power (=). These three powers then have to be understood as valences that determine the actuality of a movement. This actuality of a movement is known in Trialectics as the *function* that can be found in two possible forms—as the *function* of one or unity, or as the *function* of two or multiplicity. This corresponds to the Platonic elements of same and different or in Neoplatonism as 'the one and the many,' and in Protoanalysis, these Elements become the two Poles, to which we will refer later.

Thus Integralism considers a set of three Elements, the dynamic

Elements of every movement in the Cosmos as well as in the human psyche or the microcosm, and a set of two functional Elements that have a relation of polarity or opposition. In this polarity exists the fundamental function of the 'will to live,' which is at the very basis of life; it is moved by the three dynamic Elements because that will or that intention to live and survive manifests with three different valences. This will or intention, because it produces an imbalance in the internal life of the Cosmos, becomes the ultimate foundation of what is discordant and unstable, producing basic suffering in the sense of always feeling incomplete and needy. Thus the actual content of the Cognitive Mind (Sphere 17) is the will or the intention to survive, manifesting as suffering which becomes, following the Integral Theory, the monad that will develop into an internal triad because of the three dynamics, which then appear as three triads which form an ennead (enneagram). In this way the content of the Cognitive Mind (Sphere 17) is the Enneagram of Suffering, as the most basic premise of human existence. Lord Gautama defined life as suffering. In Integralism the basic function of life becomes a tension and this tension becomes suffering because of the internal movement which is the intention or 'will to live.'

Thus suffering (point 9), as a monad, evolves into desire (point 3) and desire into fear (point 6) which is the central triad of the Enneagram of Suffering. In the Being Group, suffering (point 9) falls into defilement (point 8) and continues into depression (point 1). These three points are related to the Conservation Instinct. The Living Group has as its central point desire (point 3) which falls into ignorance (point 2) and continues into anxiety (point 4) which together relate to the Relation Instinct. The Doing Group starts in fear (point 6), falls into distraction (point 5), and continues into stress (point 7) which relates to the Adaptation Instinct. The movement of the three dynamics is studied following the second Law of Trialectics which establishes the Law of Circulation of everything in the Cosmos, external or internal, in accordance with the valence or forces.

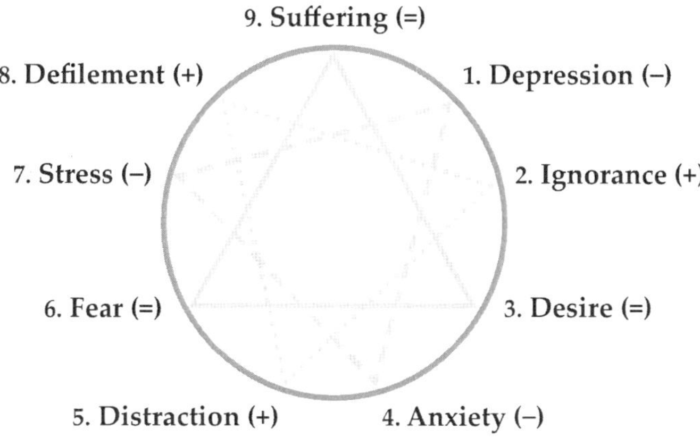

DYNAMIC ENNEAGRAM OF SUFFERING

We know that by working with the Divine Forms following the Law of Mutation or change, it is possible to dissolve the Fixations at the level of the Existential Mind (Sphere 15). In the same way, by working with the Divine Forms, following the pattern set by the Dynamic Enneagram of Suffering, it is possible to work with the most basic root of suffering and thus liberate our psyche from the most profound suffering, desire and fear, as well as their consequences.

The Dynamic Enneagram of Suffering shows us that there are internal triads that correspond to the same dynamics or

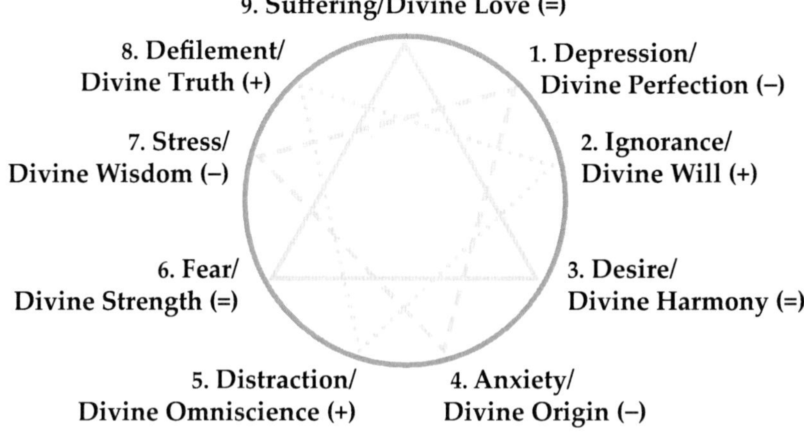

DYNAMIC ENNEAGRAM OF INTEGRATION, SUFFERING AND DIVINE FORMS

valences. Therefore, the *result* valence (substantial/Plato) corresponds to points 9, 3 and 6. The *action* valence corresponds to points 8, 2 and 5. The *reaction* valence corresponds to points 1, 4 and 7. In this way, suffering, desire and fear are the *result* moment; defilement, ignorance and distraction are the *action* moment; and depression, anxiety and stress are the *reaction* moment.

By working upon the same pattern with the Divine Forms—where Divine Love, Divine Harmony, and Divine Strength are the *result* (substantial/Plato); Divine Truth, Divine Will, and Divine Omniscience are the *action* moment; and Divine Perfection, Divine Origin, and Divine Wisdom are the *reaction* aspects—it is possible to see each of these triads becoming a Unity (*result*) again. This is possible because they follow the same valence or they have the same type of force. In this way, it is possible to neutralize the 'valence in itself' and thus effect the Unity of the triads by following their mutual discovery and obvious mutual internal definition.

For example, the *reaction* or lower aspects of the triad of depression, anxiety and stress can be observed as being psychically subjective and a *reaction*, in the sense that these aspects tend to paralyze, minimize and reduce the movement, amplifying the suffering in the direction of a damp, dark suffering, full of misery, solitude, and lower manifesting emotions. With the same analysis, we can observe the *action* and aggressive aspects of the triad of defilement, ignorance and distraction. Here the suffering of defilement is in respect to our past mistakes about which we feel guilt and remorse, which increases our state of ignorance and of being subjected to a fate over which we have no will or control because we do not know what it is and we are completely ignorant about it. The suffering of ignorance continues into a distraction that is our way to deal with this suffering of ignorance; it is in the suffering of distraction or the seeking of entertainment and all sorts of escapism where the *active* triad finishes. The substantial triad of suffering, desire and fear is the substance of suffering which evolves into desire, as in the very basic example that if I suffer any pain, I desire health; if I suffer poverty, I desire riches; and this desire will continue and evolve into fear. Thus, we fear poverty because we fear that we will not attain our desires. What we learn from working the dynamic triads or the points of the same valence is that, by working with them, we learn and come to discover much deeper definitions because the triads have the same dynamic valence and interrelations. Because the Divine Forms are the right antidote to the nine different forms of suffering, when working with the pattern of the Dynamic Enneagram of Suffering, we can transcend the deepest of all the lower Levels of Consciousness and the root of basic suffering that permeates our entire life. In the same way, as suffering is the monad of the Enneagram of Suffering, Divine Love is the monad of the Enneagram of Divine Forms and thus, in one look, this Divine Form is the transformation or, even better, the transmutation of suffering into Divine Love.

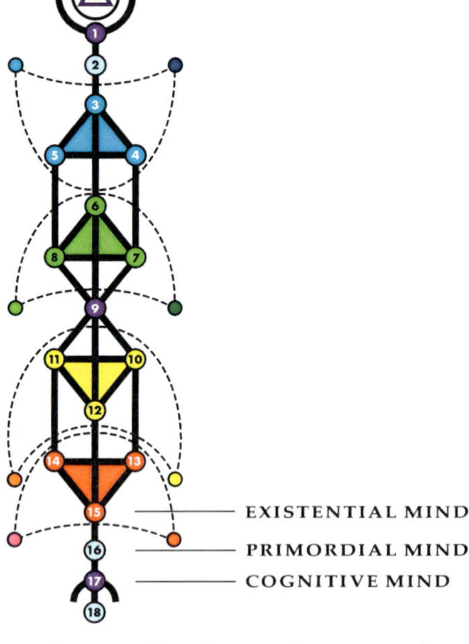

In accordance with Integralism, the three deepest forms of consciousness, perception and experience of the human psyche are disclosed in the Cognitive Mind (Sphere 17) with the five basic Elements and the Dynamic Enneagram of Suffering as its content. The Primordial Mind (Sphere 16) follows with the two Poles as its content, and then we find the Existential Mind (Sphere 15) with the Enneagram of the Fixations as its content. These three most basic levels of consciousness, perception and experience of our psyche, with their most basic problems of suffering, duality and attachment, have to be dissolved since they are the three most dense obscurations, and consequently the basis and root of our entire individual and personal psychic system. The obscuration of attachment is clarified by dissolving the Fixations which, in their essence, are nine forms of ego–attachments. With that purpose, it is possible to follow the first Law of Trialectics, the Law of Process (Law of Mutation) which considers a complete cycle. Then we work with the Enneagram of Suffering which is the content of the Cognitive Mind (Sphere 17), which is possible to dissolve and liberate by following the Law of Circulation, the second Law of Trialectics or the law of the triads and their internal valences or dynamics by way of the Enneagram of Integration. By recognizing the pattern of the same valences, we can attain the liberation from the valences themselves, and thus transcend the movement and contingency of the basic suffering. By working with the Divine Forms following the same pattern, it is possible to transmute the dynamics of suffering into the realization of the Divine Forms and Divine Transcendental Love.

Yet, from the triad of the most basic problems of suffering, duality and attachment, what is left for us to see is the problem of duality, which appears in its full manifestation in the Primordial Mind (Sphere 16) with its content of the Spiritual and Sexual Poles. In accordance with the Integral Theory, the two Poles are the two functional ways in which the most basic 'will to live' manifests itself by way of generation and continuation of life by sexual activity and by the continuation through life in the Spirit beyond death and attaining Transcendental Immortality.

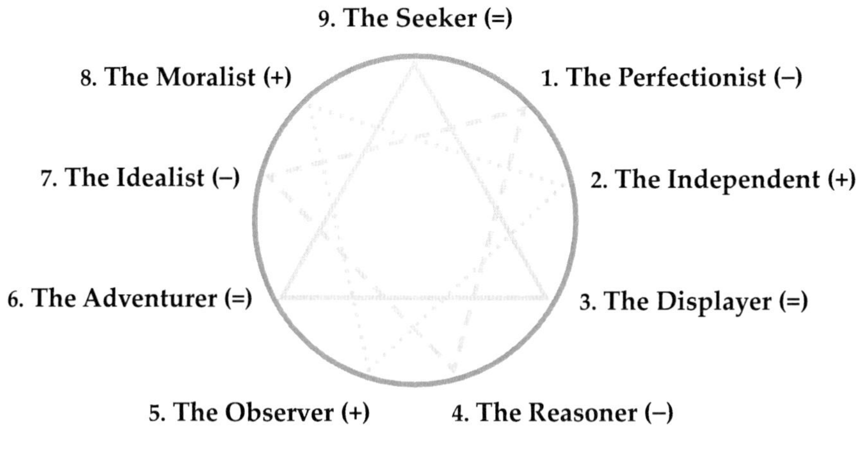

ENNEAGRAM OF ORIENTATION
THIRD LAW OF TRIALECTICS: LAW OF ATTRACTION

Thus, at the very beginning of our psychic life, we are confronted with the polarity of body and Spirit which produces the basic separation between what is material and what is spiritual, the fundamental duality that confuses our life and conceals the Ultimate Union and Oneness of all. This most basic duality of matter and Spirit can be dissolved by working with the Divine Forms across the Enneagram of Orientation, which follows the third Law of Trialectics—the Law of Attraction toward The One or the same, or toward the multiple or the different.

By way of the Dynamic Enneagram of Integration (Second Law of Trialectics, Law of Circulation), we can integrate all the points of the enneagram into the original monad. When the Divine Forms explain each other, they produce a higher understanding, so to speak, and each one of the Divine Forms appears as a manifestation of the Enneagram of the Integration of the Pure Lights, which is the content of the Crystalline State of the Ornamental Mind (Sphere 3), where the nine Pure Forms of Innate Awareness are realized.

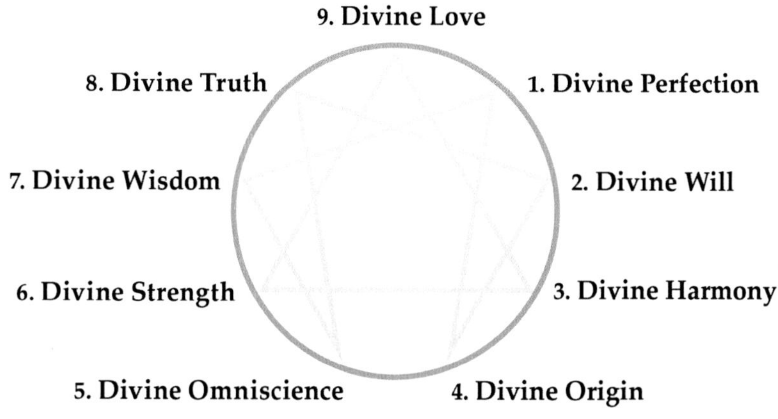

ENNEAGRAM OF THE DIVINE FORMS

The Enneagram of the Integration of the Pure Lights is composed of: (1) Completeness, (2) Luminosity, (3) Openness, (4) Transparency, (5) Intelligence, (6) Awareness, (7) Awakening, (8) Wholeness, and (9) Oneness. In order to produce the integration between the points of this enneagram, it is necessary to work with triads of specific points with different valences. When the meditation of understanding the three points has been produced, a clear State of Enlightenment as a pure and perfect experience of a Pure Divine Light is attained. Thus, the unitive experience of the three Divine Forms becomes an actual visionary experience of intensified Light at the same time that we understand its profound and alive meaning.

First, we start with Divine Love (point 9), which is neutral, then we move to Divine Omniscience (point 5), and then conclude in Divine Perfection (point 1). This pattern completes this triad and a State of Contemplation appears with a total sense of the Pure Light of Completeness or Perfection. The next triad starts with Divine Perfection (point 1), continues to Divine Strength

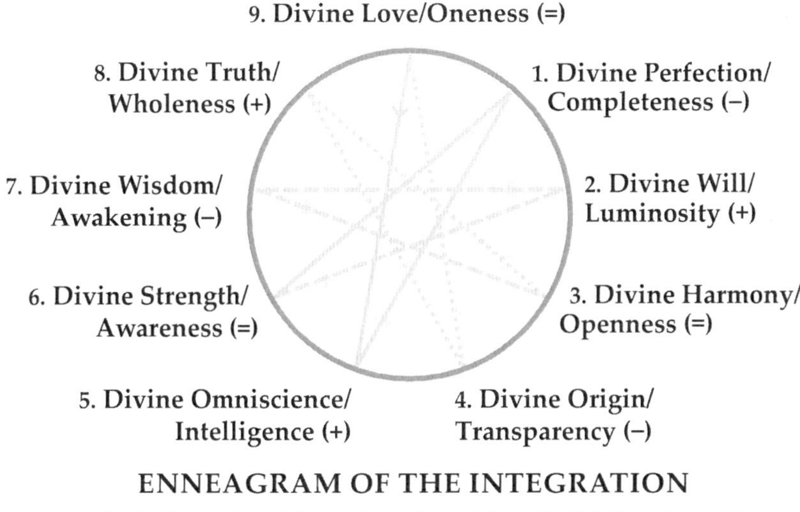

ENNEAGRAM OF THE INTEGRATION OF THE PURE LIGHTS OF THE DIVINE FORMS

(point 6), and finishes in Divine Will (point 2), which opens the Pure Light of Luminosity. Third, we start with Divine Will (point 2), move to Divine Wisdom (point 7), and then finish in Divine Harmony (point 3), and we enter the Pure Light of Openness. Next we start in Divine Harmony (point 3), move to Divine Truth (point 8), and we finish in Divine Origin (point 4), where we experience the Pure Light of Transparency. Fifth, we start with Divine Origin (point 4) which opens Divine Love (point 9), and we finish in Divine Omniscience (point 5), where we realize the Pure Light of Intelligence. Next we start with Divine Omniscience (point 5), which opens Divine Perfection (point 1), and we finish in Divine Strength (point 6), which opens the Pure Light of Innate Awareness. Seventh, we start with Divine Strength (point 6), move to Divine Will (point 2), and we finish in Divine Wisdom (point 7), in which we experience the Pure Light of Awakening. Next we start with Divine Wisdom (point 7), move to Divine Harmony (point 3), and we finish in Divine Truth (point 8), in which we discover the Pure Light of Wholeness. Finally, we start with Divine Truth (point 8), move to Divine Origin (point 4), and we finish with Divine Love (point 9), where we experience the Pure Light of Oneness.

CHAPTER 6

CONCLUSION

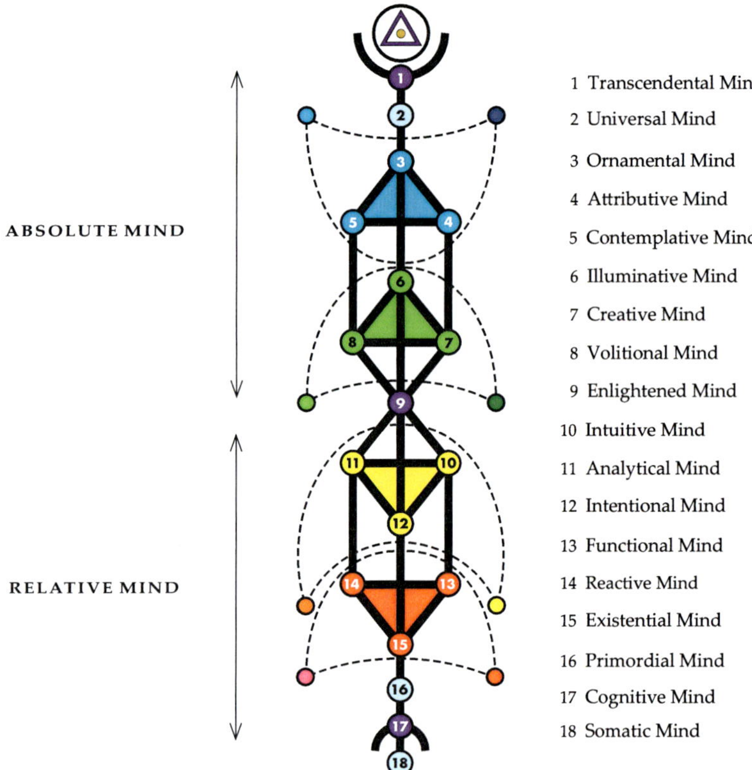

THE SCARAB

Integral Philosophy advances doctrines in theoretical form and presents practices for the actual embodiment of the theoretical propositions and the clarification of the psyche. After this Work of embodying the theoretical propositions and clarification, we can say that 'Integral Philosophy in itself' is completed by contemplation and transcendental practices. The philosophical part of Integralism is studied by taking Trialectics as its methodology, the eighteen Spheres of The Scarab as the structure and basis of the entire human psyche, and Protoanalysis as the way for clarifying the Relative Mind process. Because these series of minds are related hierarchically, once they are exposed in their Totality, it is possible to integrate them in such a way as to make order of the diverse elements of our psyche, and consequently they serve as an effective ladder of Knowledge by which we can integrate our entire spiritual life with all the levels of human existence.

The Divine Forms, as exposed in this book, correspond to the Creative Mind (Sphere 7), and by entering into the living Innate Awareness of these Forms it is possible to unite with the Pleroma of the Eternal Presence, the attainment of the State of Pristine Enlightenment (*Theosis*).

THE DIVINE FORMS AND THE SYSTEM OF THE SCARAB

As I said at the beginning of this book, the Divine Forms have to be taken in a strict Platonic sense. This is to say that they are transcendental to our material perception and cognition. Because of this characteristic of transcendentality, the Divine Forms cannot be disclosed or perceived by a mind of relativity or a Relative Mind of Concepts and Language, since this mind is completely dependent on pure materiality for its meanings, characteristics and composition.

However, the Divine Forms are presented as intellectual concepts and, as such, have no value of transcendentality because intellectual concepts are attached to materiality and our ordinary reality which is contingent and ever–changing. Thus the word–concept that defines the Form has to be filled with approximate meaning in the sense of guidance or perhaps of targeting a certain precise goal. This guidance is by way of a Trialectical Analysis of forces and by the linear analysis of processes which provide depth to the Mentational Analysis of the Divine Forms and also to the linear analysis of ego–reduction in order to understand the Divine Forms at the level of subjectivity and materiality. This effort to dematerialize the word–concepts into pure meaning becomes actualized when first the Enlightened Mind (Sphere 9) has been opened by way of attention, concentration, meditation, contemplation, and vision.

As previously said, the System of The Scarab is composed of nine Spheres corresponding to the Absolute Mind and nine Spheres corresponding to the Relative Mind. The ninth Sphere is the center of the entire System, the point of unification or harmonization of the Absolute and Relative Minds by entering into the Innate Awareness that both are one and the same. Though they have a completely different presentation, they are in fact of the same nature and Unity. When this Unity is attained in any sort of contemplative Transcendence, the Divine Immortal Aspect of our Divine Spiritual Consciousness becomes awakened, opening the realm of perfect Enlightenment or realization of The Truth, which opens the Transcendental Mind of Enlightenment, the Ornamental Mind.

In accordance with the metaphysics of Integralism, once the Ornamental Mind has been disclosed and, in fact, we have entered into a Transcendental Innate Awareness that observes and perceives Reality in absolute terms or a completeness of view that sees everything as a reflection of the clear mirror of the Mind, we enter into a State of Pure Enlightenment. This State happens in Sphere 1 of the Ornamental State and is unchangeable and Eternal. In short, once we attain The State by a true experience of Transcendence, The State stays with us forever and there is nothing to perfect in it since it is a Total Completion or a Great Perfection, over which there is nothing else. Nevertheless, paradoxical as it is, every time we re–experience the State of Enlightened Transcendentality or the Ornamental Mind, the State of Enlightenment appears to be more mature, more full of internal meaning and realization which cannot be translated into words because it is an experience of Pure Absolute Mind or Divine Spirit which is the Eternal Presence in the middle of our heart.

Thus, this Innate Awareness that happens in the Realm of the Spirit will never abandon us; it opens for us true Liberation from the materiality of the relative world which ties us in its mesh of contingent and perishable realities. Therefore, the awakening of the Spirit by Way of Enlightenment or the positing of the Ornamental Mind, once experienced, will never be forgotten, opening for us a true passage into immortality, as from the Spirit to the Spirit or the Divine into the Divine. In Integral Philosophy, we enter into the enlightened Ornamental Mind by way of different approaches or special ways of contemplation and *Theosis* (Enlightenment). The main contemplative practices are listed in the website of the Arica School (www.arica.org) under Transcendental State Trainings.

Once the Ornamental Mind of Pristine Enlightenment has been attained, having been realized in the realm of Pure Innate Awareness, it is permanent and imperishable, however unaware we are of the Transcendental State when in our ordinary awakened life. But since it is necessary to clarify and order all the Levels of our psyche with Knowledge and experience, the ordering and understanding of them makes our return to the State of Happiness and Bliss of the Ornamental Mind not only much easier, but logically inevitable. This is why, in the Protoanalytic System, working with the Poles, Instincts, Levels, Functions, and the Domains is indispensable for the clarification necessary in order to attain a full and total realization in the Absolute and Transcendental (Spheres 9–1) of The Scarab. It is by this means that all the Spheres of the Relative Mind (Spheres 18–10), because they have been clarified and ordered, give rise to the Enlightened Mind (Sphere 9), which acquires a permanency through all our ordinary awakened states, now seen from the point of view of the Absolute Mind. And also by entering into the disclosure of the Spheres of the Absolute Mind, we attain a paradoxical enlargement of the enlightened Ornamental Mind. This is precisely what happens while working with the Divine Energies, the Divine Forms, the Integral Virtues, the Divine Principles of Negative Theology, the Divine Attributes, the Divine Gnoses, the Divine Names of God, and the Divine Metatelos Deity and His Pleroma (*Theosis*) at the end of The Scarab Meditations. The State of *Theosis* is also worked at the end of the practice of *Divine Nature*. Then what we attain by working with the Divine Forms is this transcendental enlargement and further discovery of meaning beyond concepts and language.

The outcome of these contemplations is the empowering of pure meaning or 'comprehensions' by which we enter into a deeper Innate Awareness of the Divine Forms, however paradoxical it may seem, since the Divine Forms in themselves are Perfect, Eternal and unchanging in a strict Platonic sense.

WE ARE ONE

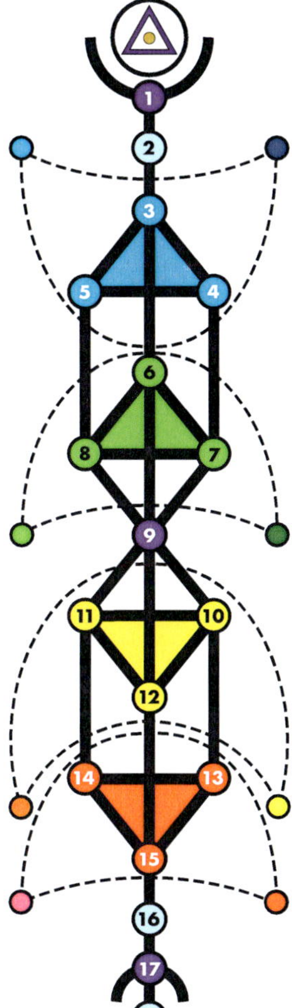

THE SCARAB

OSCAR ICHAZO
1931–2020

Oscar lchazo is the originator of the new tradition of Integral Philosophy, which presents a complete analysis of the human condition from the lowest levels of subjectivity up to the Highest States of Enlightenment (Gk. *Theosis*). In 1968 he founded the Arica School of Knowledge, through which he presented the Enneagrammatic Theory of Protoanalysis (first analysis) as well as its Theoretical Teachings and Practices.

From the beginning Ichazo's Teachings answered three most important metaphysical questions: What is humankind? What is the Supreme Good of humanity? What is the Truth that gives meaning and value to human life? His work also includes the Universal Truths supported by a new logic of cycles called "Trialectics," the logical Laws of the Mind in the 'process of becoming.'

Ichazo wrote numerous books and training manuals (group trainings, individual trainings, and meditational practices), for over fifty-five years. The Oscar Ichazo Foundation was established to support the publications endeavor and is the nonprofit organization in which the copyrights of the Integral Philosophical Knowledge are held, including the teachings and trainings into the Higher States of attainment. The Arica School, through Arica Institute Training Sponsors, has presented Ichazo's live group trainings of Protoanalysis and other related teachings worldwide.

Ichazo died at his home on Maui, Hawai'i in 2020 at the age of 88, and is survived by Sarah, his wife of 40 years, who, with many friends and students of the Arica School, continues to offer Ichazo's Teachings for the benefit of all and the realization of a united humanity (Humanity- One).

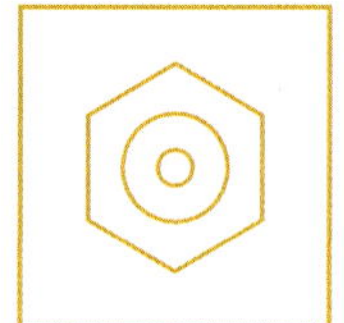

The Human Process for Enlightenment and Freedom: A Series of Five Lectures (1975) (out of print)

Psychocalisthenics (1976) (out of print)

Between Metaphysics and Protoanalysis: A Theory for Analyzing the Human Psyche (1982) (revised 2024; *The Enneagram in Five Lectures)*

Interviews with Oscar Ichazo (1982) (in revision)

Master Level Exercise: Psychocalisthenics (1986) (revised 2024; *Make Exercise A Meditation, Mastering Your Breath)*

Letters to the School (1988)

Kath State: The Energy of Inner Fire (2004)

P–Cals/Psychocalisthenics: Exercises to Awaken Your Core Fire (2011)

Core Fire: Awaken • Generate • Revitalize (2012)

Human Culture and Enlightenment (2015)

Oscar Ichazo: Insights into the Teacher • The Philosophy • The School (2015)

The Religious Consciousness (2016)

A Commentary on Protoanalysis (2018)

The Nine Constituents: The Science of the Human Condition from Ego to Enlightenment (2018)

The Four Killers of Humanity (2020)

The History of the Integral Teachings, Volume One (2020)

Letters, The Ultimate Purpose of the Arica School, Beyond Plagiarism and Misuse (2020)

We Are One, Facing our Global Crisis with Unity (2021)

Parallels between Platonism and Mahayana Buddhism (2023)

A Commentary on Crazy Wisdom (2023)

The Enneagrams of the Fixations, The Original Teachings (2023)

The Enneagrams of Ethics • Virtues • Senses—The Original Integral Teachings (2024)

Oscar Ichazo: Insights into the Teacher • The Philosophy • The School • The Enneagram (2024)

The Enneagram in Five Lectures (2024)

Enneagram Knowledge, Teachings by Oscar Ichazo (2024)

The Climate Catastrophe—The Four Killers, Beyond Eco-Anxiety into Unity and Action (extended version of We Are One, Facing our Global Crisis with Unity) (2024)

Making Exercise A Meditation, Mastering Your Breath (2024)

The History of the Integral Teachings, Volume Two (2025)

THE ARICA SCHOOL

The Arica School is a School of Knowledge founded in 1968 by Oscar Ichazo that presents a contemporary method for the clarification of the human process, establishing the ground of Unity for entering into States of Enlightenment and true Liberation for the benefit of all humanity.

THE OSCAR ICHAZO FOUNDATION

The Oscar Ichazo Foundation is a nonprofit foundation with the sole purpose of developing and producing the publications, and the group and individual trainings of Oscar Ichazo for the Arica School and the public at large. These include the complete Teachings of Integral Philosophy, the Protoanalytical trainings and Teachings, and the "Theory of the Fixations" of which he was the originator.

To contact the Foundation, email:
orders@theoscarichazofoundation.org

To contact the Arica School, email:
orders@arica.org

BOOKS AND TRAININGS BY OSCAR ICHAZO

store.arica.org and www.amazon.com

WE ARE ONE TRAINING

www.weareonetraining.org

THE ARICA SCHOOL

www.arica.org